HUGH CARPENTER & TERI SANDISON

Hot Chicken

TEN SPEED PRESS

TEN SPEED PRESS
Post Office Box 7123
Berkeley, California 94707

Cover and interior design by Beverly Wilson
Typography by Jeff Brandenburg/ImageComp
Typefaces used in this book are Avant Garde and Van Dijk.

Library of Congress Cataloging-in-Publication Data
Carpenter, Hugh.
Hot chicken / Hugh Carpenter & Teri Sandison.
        p.   cm.
Includes index.
ISBN 0-89815-771-4 (paper)
1. Cookery (Chicken)   I. Sandison, Teri.   II. Title.
TX750.5.C45C37   1995
641.6'65 — dc20   95-16344
                                CIP

First printing 1995
Printed in China
1 2 3 4 5 — 99 98 97 96 95

We dedicate this book to
our friend and publisher, Phil Wood,
gator wrestler, patron of the arts,
and friend to chefs and authors.

"Contents"

Hot Chicken Night After Night

There are few greater sensory delights than the aroma and sound of chicken roasting in the oven; the sight of golden, crisp batter-fried chicken; and the taste of perfectly cooked chicken sliced and tossed with salad greens. No other food offers home cooks such a wealth of cooking options, ranging from simple soups to braised chicken bubbling in pots. Few other foods are so readily available fresh, so reasonably priced, and so easy to cook.

We assumed that chicken had always been a plentiful and inexpensive staple of the American diet. But, while chicken now accounts for almost one third of our total meat consumption, its popularity is a very recent phenomenon in America. The total broiler production of 34 million in 1934 is the amount now processed in less than one working day. Per capita consumption of chicken grew from only 9 pounds in 1950 to 37 pounds by 1970 and to 71 pounds in 1994, and is projected by the chicken industry to exceed 85 pounds per capita by the year 2000. When inflation is accounted for in the retail price of chicken today, the cost is less than one fourth of what it was in the 1950s.

If health is your primary concern, chicken is a wise choice. A 3-ounce serving of roasted chicken breast, without the skin, contains only 116 calories (compared with 165 calories for 3 ounces of trimmed and broiled steak and 173 for 3 ounces of pork chops), but provides over half of one day's protein requirement. For a 2,000-calorie-per-day diet, that same 3-ounce serving of chicken breast contains only 2 percent of the recommended maximum total fat intake, 2 percent of the recommended maximum total sodium intake, and 24 percent of the recommended maximum cholesterol intake. In addition, chicken is a good source of iron, riboflavin, niacin, phosphorous, and potassium.

We have found that some of life's warmest moments occur around the dinner table when we're sharing good food and conversation with family and friends. The recipes in this book use everyday equipment, simple preparation steps, and common cooking techniques to achieve superb food. Surround sautéed chicken with a brilliantly colored tangerine glaze; roast tequila-marinated chicken, then nap (coat) it with a sauce of chiles and goat cheese; or simmer chicken with shiitake and portobello mushrooms to create a masterpiece when entertaining. Quick salads are accented with cold roasted chicken, soups sizzle with the addition of stir-fried chicken, and easy marinades work magic with barbecued chicken. Whether the chicken is roasted with an intensely fresh-tasting lemon glaze or simmered with allspice, ginger, and chile, it is ideal for our fast-paced lives.

Join us in an exciting culinary adventure, and let chicken play a starring role in your kitchen night after night.

Hugh Carpenter and Teri Sandison

Cool Chicken Salads and Hot Chicken Soups

*I*n this chapter you will see chicken reveal its versatility, its ease of preparation, and its unique ability to provide a perfect medium for flavors from around the world. Whether you stir-fry chicken breasts to toss with salad greens glistening with a tropical dressing, add barbecued chicken from a previous night's meal to a Caribbean soup, or combine perfectly poached chicken with toasted almonds and crisp rice sticks for a classic Chinese chicken salad, the recipes in this chapter will make you a cooking star.

Salads

These salad recipes show you how to take the simple ingredients of chicken and salad greens and transform them into exceptional taste sensations. Chicken breasts poached in water, then "shocked" in an ice-water bath (as in the recipe for Chinese Chicken Salad with Hazelnuts) are more moist than chicken cooked by any other technique. Chicken breasts straight from the barbecue, quickly sliced, and tossed with salad greens (as in the recipe for Chicken Salad with Sweet Grilled Pears) make a dramatic chicken salad with a rainbow of varying colors, textures, and tastes. For less last-minute work, marinate chicken pieces with a little of the salad dressing, roast or barbecue the chicken, and cut the meat into bite-sized pieces hours in advance of serving (as in the recipe for Thai Tropical Chicken Salad). Combine already cooked chicken with available greens or noodles for the Smoked Chicken Salad with Candied Nuts or Tandoori Noodle Salad. Or crown salad greens with wok-seared chicken for a simple work-night entrée. By mixing and matching chicken cooked by various techniques with your own favorite blend of salad greens and dressings, you'll transform the common into taste sensations.

Soups

As you read through the recipes, remember how easy it is to vary the techniques. Chicken stir-fried and transferred blazing hot from the wok to a bowl of soup could easily substitute for the barbecued chicken in Caribbean Chicken Soup. If you love the intense chicken flavor of Wild Mushroom Gumbo Soup, which results from browning chicken pieces and then simmering them in soup, use the same technique to make Tortilla Chicken Soup Olé! If you are able to purchase whole smoked chickens from a local grower, save the bones and use them for simmering and thus enriching the flavor of any soup. Finally, all these flavor-intense soups yield show-stopping results, even when substituting barbecued or roasted chicken from last night's dinner.

Chicken Salad with Sweet Grilled Pears

Chicken and fruit are natural flavor partners, and this is particularly true when they are cooked together on the barbecue. In this "artful" main-course salad, grilled pears achieve a complex taste as sugars caramelize with the high heat of the barbecue. Crisp, moist, sweet, and hot, they are a dramatic foil to strips of barbecued chicken and toasted pecans. Be sure to keep the chicken and pear marinades separate, and use two pastry brushes—one for brushing on the chicken marinade and the second for brushing on the pear marinade.

Serves 4 as an entrée

SALAD DRESSING

6 tablespoons walnut oil or extra virgin olive oil

¼ cup balsamic vinegar

¼ cup freshly squeezed orange juice

2 tablespoons honey

½ teaspoon Asian or Caribbean chile sauce

½ teaspoon salt

1 clove garlic, finely minced

¼ cup loosely packed cilantro sprigs, freshly chopped

INGREDIENTS

4 chicken breast halves, boned but skin on

2 Anjou pears

1 cup pecan halves

8 cups baby greens or torn mixed lettuce

ADVANCE PREPARATION

Preheat the oven to 325 degrees to toast the pecans. In a small jar, combine the salad dressing ingredients. Rinse the chicken breasts with cold water, then pat dry. Trim all excess fat from around the edges. Place the chicken on a small plate, shake the dressing well, then add ¼ cup of the dressing to marinate the chicken. Cover and refrigerate the chicken for at least 10 minutes but not longer than 8 hours.

Cut each pear into 8 wedges (do not peel), then cut out the core. Place the pears in a bowl, shake the salad dressing, and add ¼ cup of the dressing to marinate the pears. Cover and refrigerate the pears at least 10 minutes but not longer than 8 hours.

Place the pecans on a baking sheet, and toast them in the preheated oven for 15 minutes, stirring midway through toasting, then set them aside. Wash and thoroughly dry the greens. *All advance preparation steps may be completed up to 8 hours before you begin the final cooking steps.*

FINAL COOKING STEPS

If using a gas barbecue or indoor grill, preheat to medium (350 degrees). If using charcoal or wood, prepare a fire. When the gas barbecue or indoor grill is heated or the coals or wood is ash covered, brush the cooking rack with oil, then lay the chicken in the central, hottest part of the rack and the pears around the outside of the chicken. Grill the chicken for about 2 minutes on each side. The chicken is done when an instant-read meat thermometer registers 150° and the juices run clear when the chicken is pierced with a fork. As the chicken cooks, brush on all the remaining chicken marinade. Grill the pears until they are heated through and soften slightly, about 2 minutes on each side. Using a clean pastry brush that has not touched the chicken marinade, brush the pears with the remaining pear marinade.

Transfer the chicken and pears to a cutting board. Place the greens in a large bowl. Shake the remaining salad dressing and toss with the greens. Divide the dressed greens among 4 dinner plates. Cut the chicken into thin slices. Position the chicken slices, grilled pears, and pecans on top of the greens. Serve at once.

SUGGESTED ACCOMPANIMENTS

Spicy California corn bread muffins and ginger ice cream with chocolate crisp cookies

The deep low notes of barbecued chicken provide a dramatic contrast to the sweet, high notes of tropical fruits. In order to provide a perfect match of flavors, a portion of the salad dressing is used as the marinade/barbecue sauce for the chicken. While we like the contrasts of both dark and white meat in this salad, it is also excellent with barbecued, grilled, or roasted chicken breast meat. Other variations include adding 4 cups of torn or baby greens during the final combining of ingredients, and widening the range of fruits to include raspberries, strawberries, kiwis, and baby bananas.

Serves 4 as an entrée

Thai Tropical Chicken Salad

INGREDIENTS

1½ frying chickens, cut into pieces

2 papayas, not quite ripe and still slightly firm

2 red bell peppers

½ hothouse cucumber

½ cup pine nuts

2 ripe avocados

SALAD DRESSING

1 tablespoon minced lime zest

6 tablespoons freshly squeezed lime juice

¼ cup safflower oil

¼ cup light brown sugar

¼ cup Thai fish sauce

2 teaspoons Asian or Caribbean chile sauce

2 tablespoons very finely minced ginger

2 cloves garlic, finely minced

3 tablespoons minced cilantro

ADVANCE PREPARATION

Preheat the oven to 325 degrees (to toast the nuts). Rinse the chicken with cold water, then pat dry and place in a mixing bowl. Peel, seed, and cut the papayas into ½-inch cubes. Cut off and discard the stem, ribbing, and seeds of the pepper. Cut the peppers into ½-inch cubes. Cut the cucumber into long ½-inch-wide strips, then cut across the strips to make ½-inch cubes. Place the papayas, peppers, and cucumber in a bowl and refrigerate. Place the pine nuts on a baking sheet and toast in the preheated oven until golden, about 8 minutes; set aside the pine nuts. Set aside the avocados.

In a small jar, combine the salad dressing ingredients. Shake vigorously. Pour half the dressing over the chicken for the chicken marinade, turn the pieces over to coat them, cover, and refrigerate the chicken for at least 15 minutes but no longer than 8 hours. Set aside the other half of the salad dressing.

To barbecue the chicken: If using a gas barbecue, preheat to medium (350 degrees). If using charcoal or wood, prepare a fire. When the gas barbecue is heated or the coals or wood is ash covered, brush the cooking rack with oil, then lay the chicken pieces in the center of the rack. Grill the chicken for about 12 minutes on each side. The chicken is done when an instant-read meat thermometer registers 170 degrees when inserted deeply into a thigh and the juices run clear when the chicken is pierced with a fork. As the chicken cooks, brush on all the remaining chicken marinade.

Let the chicken pieces cool to room temperature, remove the meat from the bone, cut it into bite-sized pieces, and refrigerate. *All of the advance preparation steps may be completed up to 8 hours before you begin the final cooking steps.*

FINAL ASSEMBLY STEPS

Seed and cut the avocados into ½-inch cubes. If the chicken has been refrigerated, bring back to room temperature. In a large bowl, combine the avocados, papayas, peppers, and cucumber. Shake the salad dressing and toss it with the fruit and vegetable mixture. Place the salad on 4 dinner plates. Place the chicken pieces on top of the salad, sprinkle with the pine nuts, and serve at once.

SUGGESTED ACCOMPANIMENTS

Garlic Parmesan bread, chilled asparagus with fresh herb dressing, and coconut crème brûlée

Types of Chicken

All the recipes in this book use broiler-fryer chickens, a type of chicken available at virtually every market in North America. These are young, tender chickens, 7 weeks old and weighing 2 to 4 pounds. Excellent barbecued, grilled, roasted, broiled, sautéed, stir-fried, and braised in liquid, broiler-fryers are sold whole, split into halves, cut into pieces, or packaged by sections (breasts, legs, thighs, drumsticks, and wings). For information about other types of chickens available to home cooks, see "Hot Chicken Sage Advice," page 89.

Cooking Times

Cooking chicken perfectly requires careful attention. The moment chicken loses its pink color next to the bone or in the center of boneless pieces, it is perfectly cooked. The United States Department of Agriculture recommends cooking whole chicken to an internal temperature of 180 degrees, bone-in parts to 170 degrees, and boneless chicken to 160 degrees. We think this results in noticeably dry meat, and prefer to cook whole chicken, whole legs, thighs, and drumsticks to 170 degrees, bone-in chicken breasts to 155 degrees, and boneless chicken breasts (both skin-on and skinless) to 150 degrees. Always err on the side of safety: If you are not sure that chicken has been cooked until all its pink color has disappeared, cook it longer.

We find the best way to determine whether chicken has been perfectly cooked is to use an instant-read meat thermometer and a fork. Instant-read meat thermometers are available at all cookware shops and most hardware stores. Insert the end of the thermometer into the deepest part of the meat (the thigh, if cooking a whole chicken), and wait approximately 20 seconds for the gauge to stop moving. Don't let the end of the thermometer touch the bone, which will cause an inaccurate reading. Instant-read meat thermometers are not designed to withstand high oven heat and will break if left in the oven. Unfortunately, these thermometers also can be inaccurate. In addition to using a thermometer, we always pierce chicken meat with a fork: When the chicken is done, the juices should run clear, with no tinge of pink.

Hot Chicken Basics

While this salad uses barbecued tandoori chicken, you can easily simplify the recipe by substituting any barbecued, grilled, or roasted chicken that has been cooked as far ahead as 1 day in advance of serving. Try this as an appetizer, a small first course, part of a picnic feast, or as the main entrée for lunch. Soba noodles, sold by Japanese and other Asian markets, are made from buckwheat flour, which gives the noodles a nutty flavor and marvelous texture.

Serves 4 to 6 as an appetizer or as a small salad course

Tandoori Noodle Salad

I N G R E D I E N T S

1 cooked Tandoori Chicken (page 43)

Salt

4 ounces spaghetti or soba noodles

1 tablespoon cooking oil

1 large vine-ripened tomato

1 large carrot

1/2 hothouse cucumber

6 small red radishes

2 tablespoons white sesame seeds

S A L A D   D R E S S I N G

3 tablespoons cooking oil

1 clove garlic, finely minced

2 tablespoons very finely minced ginger

3 tablespoons thin soy sauce

3 tablespoons balsamic or white wine vinegar

2 tablespoons dark sesame oil

1 tablespoon packed light brown sugar

1 teaspoon Asian chile sauce

1/2 teaspoon finely minced orange zest

1/4 cup minced whole green onions

2 tablespoons minced cilantro sprigs

2 tablespoons minced mint leaves

ADVANCE PREPARATION

Remove the meat from the bones of the chicken, then cut the meat and any crisp chicken skin into pieces about 1 inch long and 1/4 inch wide; cover and refrigerate. Bring 4 quarts of water to a vigorous boil. Lightly salt the water and add the noodles. Cook the noodles until they are tender but still firm, about 5 minutes. Immediately drain them in a colander and rinse briefly under cold water, then shake out excess water and transfer the noodles to a bowl. Stir in the oil and set the noodles aside (you should have about 4 cups of noodles).

Cut the tomato in half and gently squeeze out the seeds; cut the tomato into thin wedges and set aside. Peel the carrot, then cut the carrot on a very sharp diagonal into 1/8-inch-thick slices; overlap the slices and cut the carrot into matchstick-shaped pieces. Place the carrot pieces in a sieve. Bring 4 cups of water to a boil, then pour the boiling water over them. Immediately transfer the carrot to a bowl of water containing a few ice cubes. When the carrot pieces are thoroughly chilled, remove pieces, pat dry, and set aside. Cut the cucumber on a sharp diagonal into 1/4-inch-thick slices, then cut the slices into 1/4-inch-thick matchstick-shaped pieces, or into narrow wedges; set aside. Trim the ends from the radishes, then cut the radishes into 1/8-inch-thick slices; set aside. In a small ungreased skillet or sauté pan, toast the sesame seeds until light golden, then transfer to a small container and set aside.

To prepare the salad dressing, place an 8-inch skillet or sauté pan over medium heat. Add the cooking oil, garlic, and ginger. Sauté the garlic until it begins to sizzle but is not brown. Immediately transfer the oil, garlic, and ginger to a small container. Add the remaining salad dressing ingredients. Stir well and set aside. *All of the above can be completed up to 8 hours before you begin the final cooking steps.*

FINAL COOKING STEPS

Place the chicken, noodles, and vegetables in a large bowl. Stir the dressing, then pour it over the noodles. Evenly combine all the ingredients and transfer the salad to a serving platter or salad plates. Sprinkle with the sesame seeds and serve at once.

SUGGESTED ACCOMPANIMENTS

East-West grilled vegetables and mango sorbet

Smoked Chicken Salad with Candied Nuts

If you can't find whole smoked chicken, double the salad dressing and marinate one raw frying chicken, cut into pieces, in half of the dressing. Cover and refrigerate for 8 hours. Barbecue the chicken in a gas barbecue over the lowest possible heat. Or place 12 to 16 lighted briquettes around the perimeter of a charcoal barbecue. At one edge of the barbecue, add a foil container holding soaked wood chips (available at home improvement centers), and keep the barbecue tightly covered to trap all the smoke. Be ready to add more moistened wood chips and lighted briquettes in order to maintain the low, steady heat and dense, smoky cooking atmosphere. Cook the chicken until the internal temperature reaches 160 degrees.

Serves 4 as an entrée

INGREDIENTS

Meat from 1 smoked chicken (approximately 1 pound)

8 cups mixed baby greens or torn mixed lettuce greens

3 ounces soft goat cheese

CANDIED NUTS

1/4 cup honey

1/4 teaspoon crushed red pepper (chile flakes)

1/4 teaspoon salt

3 tablespoons water

1/3 cup raw whole blanched almonds

1/3 cup raw whole cashews

1/3 cup raw pecan halves

SALAD DRESSING

1/3 cup extra virgin olive oil

1/4 cup white wine vinegar

1 tablespoon very finely minced ginger

2 tablespoons finely chopped basil leaves

2 tablespoons finely chopped mint leaves

1/2 teaspoon salt

ADVANCE PREPARATION

Preheat the oven to 350 degrees (to toast the nuts). Cut the chicken meat into 1-inch-long pieces about 1/2 inch wide, then cover and refrigerate. Wash and dry the lettuce and refrigerate. Crumble the goat cheese, then refrigerate.

To a small saucepan, add the honey, red pepper flakes, salt, and water. Bring to a low boil, then add the nuts. Stir the nuts slowly but continuously until all the moisture disappears. Line a baking sheet with aluminum foil or parchment paper. Spread the nuts in a single layer on the pan and place in the oven. Bake until the nuts turn a mahogany color, about 12 to 15 minutes. Remove the nuts from the oven and, when just cool enough to handle, gently break the nuts apart.

In a small jar combine salad dressing ingredients. *All advance preparation steps may be completed up to 8 hours before you begin the final cooking steps.*

FINAL ASSEMBLY STEPS

In a large bowl, combine the chicken and greens. Shake the dressing vigorously, then toss the chicken and greens with just enough of the dressing to lightly moisten them. Add the crumbled goat cheese and candied nuts and gently toss again. Transfer to salad or dinner plates and serve at once.

SUGGESTED ACCOMPANIMENTS

Asparagus soup with roasted red pepper garnish and fresh berries with chocolate Grand Marnier truffles

Chinese Chicken Salad with Hazelnuts

*S*uch is the popularity of this salad that we know of one Los Angeles restaurant that sells twenty thousand orders a year! When tossed with crisp rice sticks, field greens, and toasted nuts, the special ingredient in the dressing, red sweet ginger, creates flavor and textural contrasts sure to ignite dinner conversation. Red sweet ginger is pieces of bright red ginger in a heavy syrup, not to be confused with Japanese pickled ginger. Jars of red sweet ginger are sold by all Chinese markets (look for Mee Chun Preserved Red Ginger Slices or Koon Chun Red Ginger in Syrup); if unavailable, double the amount of finely minced ginger, and substitute an equal amount of grenadine for the syrup.

Serves 4 as an entrée

INGREDIENTS

2 whole chicken breasts, bone in and skin on

1 red bell pepper

3 small pickling cucumbers

8 cups mixed baby greens or torn mixed
   lettuce

½ cup hazelnuts

2 cups cooking oil

2 ounces rice sticks

SALAD DRESSING

3 tablespoons red wine vinegar

2 tablespoons thin soy sauce

2 tablespoons dark sesame oil

2 tablespoons juice from jar of red sweet
   ginger

1 tablespoon hoisin sauce

½ teaspoon Asian chile sauce

½ teaspoon salt

¼ cup minced red sweet ginger

2 tablespoons very finely minced ginger

¼ cup minced whole green onion

ADVANCE PREPARATION

Preheat the oven to 325 degrees (to toast the nuts). Bring 3 quarts of water to a vigorous boil and add the chicken breasts. Tightly cover the saucepan, turn off the heat, and leave the chicken breasts submerged in the gradually cooling water for 30 minutes. An instant-read meat thermometer should register 160 degrees when inserted deeply in one of the breasts. Transfer the chicken to a bowl, add 12 ice cubes, and cover the chicken with cold water. After the chicken has chilled for 20 minutes, remove and discard the skin, pull the meat off the bone, and cut the chicken into ¼-inch-thick strips. Cover and refrigerate the chicken meat.

Remove and discard the stem, ribs, and seeds from the pepper. Cut the pepper into ⅛-inch-thick strips, each about 1 inch long. Discard the stems from the cucumbers; then cut the cucumbers into ⅛-inch-thick slices; overlap the slices and cut the slices into ¼-inch-thick strips. Cover and refrigerate the pepper and cucumbers. Wash and thoroughly dry the lettuce. Place the hazelnuts on a baking sheet, and roast in a preheated 325-degree oven for 15 minutes, or until golden. If the papery skin is still on the nuts, wrap them in a kitchen towel, and let cool for a few minutes. Rub the towel vigorously between your palms until all the skins have been removed. Coarsely chop the nuts and set aside.

Add the cooking oil to a 10-inch skillet placed over medium-high heat. Heat the oil until the end of a rice stick expands within 2 seconds when placed in the oil. Pull the rice sticks apart into small bundles of approximately 10 sticks. Cook one bundle at a time. As soon as they expand, turn the rice sticks over and push them back into the hot oil to cook 2 more seconds. Drain on paper towels and store at room temperature.

Combine all the salad dressing ingredients in a small jar. *All of the advance preparation steps may be completed up to 8 hours before you begin the final cooking steps.*

FINAL ASSEMBLY STEPS

Place the chicken, pepper, cucumbers, and greens in a large salad bowl. Shake the dressing vigorously, then toss the salad ingredients with just enough dressing to lightly coat. Gently break the rice sticks into manageable lengths, then gently fold the rice sticks into the salad. Place the salad on 4 dinner plates, sprinkle toasted hazelnuts, and serve at once.

SUGGESTED ACCOMPANIMENTS

Wild rice soup and warm apricot tart

Smoked Chicken Soup with Spicy Croutons

The special flavors in this soup come from simmering chicken stock with the bones of a smoked chicken, then enriching the soup by adding fresh tarragon, smoked chicken meat, and good Spanish dry sherry. Garlic-chile croutons topped with smoked Jarlsberg cheese crown the soup. Try to purchase a whole smoked chicken rather than a smoked chicken "loaf," which is a processed chicken meat product injected with water and artificial flavors. However, if you must use processed smoked chicken (or turkey), in lieu of the chicken bones, simmer a ham hock with the chicken stock.

Serves 4 as an entrée

INGREDIENTS

1 small smoked chicken

2 yellow onions, chopped

4 cloves garlic, finely minced

¼ cup olive oil

7 cups chicken stock

½ cup wild rice, rinsed

1 bunch baby carrots (about 12)

8 spears thin asparagus

8 medium button mushrooms

3 vine-ripened tomatoes

2 tablespoons cornstarch

¼ cup fresh tarragon leaves

½ cup Spanish dry sherry

Salt and ground white pepper to taste

SPICY CROUTONS

6-inch length of very thin baguette

¼ cup olive oil

3 cloves garlic, finely minced

1 teaspoon Asian chile sauce

½ teaspoon salt

2 ounces smoked imported Jarlsberg cheese, thinly sliced

ADVANCE PREPARATION

Separate the chicken meat from the bones. Reserve the bones but discard the skin. Cut the chicken meat into soupspoon-sized pieces, cover, and refrigerate. Set aside the onion and garlic. Place a 3-quart saucepan over medium heat. Add the olive oil and the chopped onion. Sauté the onion until it is slightly brown, about 10 minutes. Add the minced garlic and sauté for 1 minute. Add the chicken bones, stock, and wild rice. Bring to a low boil, reduce the heat to low, cover the pan, and simmer for 40 minutes. After 40 minutes, remove the chicken bones, cool the soup, and cover and refrigerate if made more than 3 hours in advance of serving.

Scrub the carrots, and cut them in half on a diagonal. Snap off and discard the tough asparagus ends, then cut the asparagus on a sharp diagonal into 1-inch lengths. Cut the mushrooms into ⅛-inch-thick slices. Submerge the tomatoes into boiling water for 10 seconds, then rinse under cold water and peel away the skin. Cut the tomatoes in half and gently squeeze out the seeds, then cut the tomatoes into soupspoon-sized wedges. In separate containers, set aside the cornstarch, tarragon, and sherry.

To make croutons: Preheat the oven to 325 degrees (to toast the croutons). Cut the bread into ¼-inch-thick slices. In a small saucepan, combine the olive oil, garlic, chile sauce, and salt. Place over medium heat and cook until the garlic just begins to sizzle but has not turned brown. Immediately transfer the garlic oil mixture to a bowl, add the sliced bread, and stir the bread to evenly coat the slices on both sides. Place the bread in a single layer on a baking sheet and toast in the preheated oven until the slices are golden on both sides, about 15 minutes. Remove from the oven and cool to room temperature on the baking sheet. When cool, place thin slices of smoked cheese on the top of each crouton, then set aside the baking sheet of croutons. *All advance preparation steps may be completed up to 8 hours before you begin the final cooking steps.*

FINAL COOKING STEPS

Turn the oven setting to broil, then place the croutons in the oven and heat until the cheese melts, about 2 minutes. Finely chop the tarragon. Add 2 tablespoons cold water to the cornstarch and stir to evenly combine. Bring the soup to a low boil. Stir in the cornstarch mixture, then add the carrots, asparagus, mushrooms, tomatoes, chicken, and tarragon. Cook until the asparagus brightens. Bring the soup to a low boil. Stir in the sherry. Taste and adjust the seasoning, especially for salt. Transfer the soup to 4 heated soup bowls, top the soup with the croutons, and serve at once.

SUGGESTED ACCOMPANIMENTS

Tricolor jícama salad and Kahlúa flan

Tortilla Chicken Soup Olé

izzling chicken breasts, straight from the grill pan, sliced thinly and stirred into the soup, provide an exciting flavor and color contrast to the goat cheese, avocado, and chiles in this recipe. One of the pillars of Mexican cuisine, served by simple cafeterias and fine Mexico City restaurants, tortilla soup, has spread northward to become a favorite of American Southwest cooks. Typically made from a broth of stewed chicken, variations include using squash blossoms, chopped tomatoes, rice, or Cheddar cheese; substituting fresh oregano for the cilantro; and enriching the soup with cream. This recipe uses a solid grill pan with metal ridges in order to lightly char the vegetables and cook the chicken. Alternatively, you may char the vegetables and chicken on a gas or charcoal barbecue.

Serves 4 as an entrée

INGREDIENTS

4 chicken breast halves, boned and skinned

3 tablespoons freshly squeezed lime juice

2 tablespoons olive oil

2 tablespoons honey

1 teaspoon Asian or Mexican chile sauce

2 cloves garlic, finely minced

1 pound vine-ripened plum tomatoes, cut in half and seeded

4 poblano or 2 Anaheim chiles

2 ears white corn, husks removed

3 6-inch corn tortillas

1/3 cup cooking oil

3 ounces soft goat cheese

1/2 ripe avocado

1/4 cup cilantro sprigs

2 limes

6 cups chicken stock

Salt to taste

ADVANCE PREPARATION

Rinse the chicken with cold water, then pat dry. Cut the chicken lengthwise into long 1/2-inch-wide strips, then place in a bowl. Add the lime juice, olive oil, honey, chile sauce, and garlic; mix well. Cover and refrigerate at least 15 minutes but not longer than 8 hours.

Heat an iron grill pan over medium-high heat until very hot. Grill the tomatoes, chiles, and corn until they are lightly charred. Chop the tomatoes. Seed, stem, and cut the chiles into 1-inch-long, 1/4-inch-wide pieces. Cut the kernels off the corn. In a bowl, combine the tomatoes, chiles, and corn.

Cut the tortillas in half, then cut each half into 1/4-inch-wide strips. In a 10-inch skillet or sauté pan over medium heat, heat the cooking oil until a tortilla strip bubbles around the edges when added. Cook a few strips at a time; when golden, transfer to paper towels and drain. Crumble the goat cheese and refrigerate. *All of the above can be completed up to 8 hours before you begin the final cooking steps.*

FINAL COOKING STEPS

Within 30 minutes of serving the soup, seed the avocado. Cut the avocado into 1/4-inch-thick slices. Finely chop the cilantro. Cut the limes into wedges.

Also within 30 minutes of serving, place the grill pan over medium-high heat. Spray the grill pan with vegetable-oil cooking spray or brush with a little cooking oil. Lay the chicken strips on the grill and cook on both sides just until they lose their raw color inside, a total of about 2 minutes total cooking. Remove the chicken and cut the pieces on a sharp diagonal into 1-inch lengths.

Place the chicken stock in a 3-quart saucepan. Over medium-high heat, bring the stock to a simmer, stir in the tomatoes, chiles, and corn, and return the soup to a simmer. Stir in the chicken. Taste and adjust the seasoning, adding salt (about 2 teaspoons of salt if using homemade chicken stock). Transfer the soup to a heated soup tureen or 4 heated soup bowls. Sprinkle with the tortilla strips, crumbled goat cheese, avocado slices, and chopped cilantro. Accompany each bowl with wedges of lime. Serve at once.

SUGGESTED ACCOMPANIMENTS

Hot garlic bread, arugula salad, and vanilla bean ice cream with mango Grand Marnier sauce

This soup is a good example of Caribbean multicultural cooking, which often includes yams (or other tubers), coconut, allspice (one of the key ingredients in Jamaican jerk sauce), indigenously grown chiles, and fresh gingerroot and curry powder (introduced to the Caribbean by Indian and Chinese laborers). Adding chopped fresh cilantro, mint, and basil just before serving contributes a sparkling flavor.

Serves 4 as the entrée

Caribbean Chicken Soup

INGREDIENTS

Meat from 1 large cooked chicken (about 3 cups)

2 tablespoons cooking oil

2 tablespoons very finely minced ginger

1 tablespoon curry powder

1 large yam

2 red bell peppers

1¾ cups coconut milk

5 cups chicken stock

1 teaspoon Caribbean or Asian chile sauce

1 teaspoon ground cinnamon

½ teaspoon ground allspice

3 bay leaves

¼ cup finely chopped cilantro sprigs

¼ cup slivered mint leaves

¼ cup slivered basil leaves

Salt to taste

ADVANCE PREPARATION

Using your fingers, pull the meat away from the bones, then discard all the skin and bones. Cut the chicken meat into rectangular pieces about 1 inch long and ¼ inch thick. Place the chicken in a bowl and refrigerate.

In a small bowl, combine the oil, ginger, and curry powder. Using a potato peeler, remove the yam skin. Cut the yam crosswise into ¼-inch-thick slices. Overlap the slices and cut into ¼-inch-wide matchstick-shaped pieces. Stem, derib, and seed the peppers, then cut them into ½-inch cubes. Combine the yams and pepper and set aside. In a separate bowl, combine the coconut milk, stock, chile sauce, cinnamon, allspice, and bay leaves. *All advance preparations may be completed up to 8 hours before you begin the Final Cooking Steps.*

FINAL COOKING STEPS

In a small bowl, combine the cilantro, mint, and basil and set aside. Heat a heavy large saucepan over medium heat and add the oil, ginger, and curry powder. Sauté until the ginger sizzles and the curry powder becomes very fragrant, about 2 minutes. Add the yam and red peppers. Turn the heat to high and sauté the yam and peppers until the peppers brighten in color and the yam begins to soften, about 2 minutes.

Add the coconut milk mixture. Bring to a low simmer, then turn the heat to low and simmer the soup until the yams are tender, about 15 minutes.

Remove and discard the bay leaves. Stir in the chicken and return the soup to a simmer. Stir in the fresh herb mixture. Taste and adjust the seasoning, especially for salt and spice (add about 2 teaspoons of salt if using homemade chicken stock). Transfer to a heated soup tureen or 4 heated soup bowls. Serve at once.

SUGGESTED ACCOMPANIMENTS

Spinach, avocado, and walnut salad, garlic popovers, and flourless chocolate cake with berry purée

Hot Sour Soup with Wok-Seared Chicken

This famous soup, which is served throughout northern China, gains its dynamic range of flavors from the use of vinegar, chiles, rich chicken stock, soy, and dark sesame oil. Once preparation is completed, it takes only minutes to accomplish the final assembly. Just before serving, marinated chicken is stir-fried in a blazing hot wok or cast-iron skillet, then quickly transferred to the bowls of soup. This is a better technique than stirring raw marinated chicken into the soup, which results in rubbery meat. To encourage guests to vary the soup's flavors, place saucers of Asian chile sauce and small pitchers of balsamic, rice, or distilled vinegar on the table.

Serves 4 as an entrée

INGREDIENTS

¼ cup cilantro sprigs

3 eggs

3 tablespoons cornstarch

8 cups chicken stock

8 ounces firm bean curd (tofu)

1 carrot

1 pound green peas in the shell

3 ounces enoki mushrooms

2 whole green onions

2 tablespoons cooking oil

4 chicken breast halves, boned and skinned

SEASONING MIX

6 tablespoons distilled white vinegar

2 tablespoons dark soy sauce

2 tablespoons dark sesame oil

1 teaspoon finely and freshly ground black pepper

1 teaspoon ground white pepper

1 teaspoon Asian chile sauce

1 teaspoon salt

ADVANCE PREPARATION

In separate containers, set the cilantro, eggs, and cornstarch aside. Refrigerate the chicken stock. Cut the bean curd into ½-inch cubes or thin rectangular-shaped pieces and set aside. Peel the carrot, then cut it on a very sharp diagonal in ⅛-inch-thick slices; overlap the slices and cut them lengthwise into ⅛-inch-thick matchstick pieces. Shell the peas. Cut off the root end of the enoki mushrooms, then separate the individual mushrooms. Cut the green onions into 1-inch-long shreds. In a bowl, combine the carrot, peas, mushrooms, and green onions; cover and refrigerate. Set the cooking oil aside.

Rinse the chicken with cold water, then pat dry. Cut the chicken crosswise on a very sharp bias into the thinnest possible slices. Place the chicken in a bowl. In a small bowl, combine the seasoning mix ingredients. Add 2 tablespoons of the seasoning mix to the chicken, mix well, cover, and refrigerate. Reserve the remaining seasoning mix. *All advance preparation steps may be completed up to 8 hours before you begin the final cooking steps.*

FINAL COOKING STEPS

Place a wok over medium heat. Finely chop the cilantro. Beat the eggs until well blended. Combine the cornstarch with 3 tablespoons of water. In a 3-quart saucepan over medium-high heat, bring the chicken stock to a low boil. Stir in the bean curd. Return the soup to a low boil and stir in the cornstarch mixture. Return the soup to a low boil and stir in the vegetables. Return the soup to a low boil. Add the seasoning mix. Stir 2 tablespoons of the hot soup into the beaten eggs; then slowly pour the eggs into the soup, stirring the soup with a fork where the eggs meet the hot liquid. Taste and adjust the seasoning, especially for salt, sourness (to increase, add vinegar), and spiciness (to increase, add pepper or chile sauce).

Turn the heat to high under the wok and add the cooking oil. Immediately roll the oil around the inside of the wok and, when the oil just gives off a wisp of smoke, add the chicken. Stir and toss the chicken until it loses its raw exterior color, about 1 minute. Transfer the chicken to the soup, sprinkle on cilantro, and serve the soup at once.

SUGGESTED ACCOMPANIMENTS

Salad of field greens, crusty French bread, and chocolate brownies with peach ice cream

Wild Mushroom Gumbo Soup

Many elements from around the world form the basis for gumbo, one of the world's great soups. Starting with a French bouillabaisse, New Orleans's cooks thicken the soup by adding the African ingredient okra (in one African language the word for okra is **gumbo**). The Choctaw Indians contributed ground sassafras leaves, or filé powder, to flavor and thicken gumbo when okra was not in season. The Spanish brought rice from Europe and introduced peppers and chiles from Mexico. While this recipe uses filé powder, which is available at gourmet cookware shops, you may substitute 1 cup sliced okra, adding it to the soup when you add the green peppers.

Serves 4 as an entrée

INGREDIENTS

1 frying chicken, cut into serving pieces

½ teaspoon cayenne powder

Salt and freshly ground black pepper

½ cup unbleached all-purpose flour

¼ cup olive oil

2 yellow onions, chopped

5 cloves garlic, finely minced

1 pound fresh mushrooms (shiitakes, portobellos, chanterelles, or morels)

1 green bell pepper, stemmed, seeded, deribbed, and chopped

1 cup chopped seeded vine-ripened tomato

8 ounces andouille sausage, thinly sliced

½ cup long-grain white rice (not Minute Rice)

8 cups chicken stock

2 tablespoons Worcestershire sauce

2 tablespoons Louisiana chile sauce

4 bay leaves

¼ cup finely chopped basil leaves

2 tablespoons minced fresh thyme

2 tablespoons filé powder

ADVANCE PREPARATION

Rinse the chicken with cold water, then pat dry. Rub the chicken pieces with cayenne, a sprinkling of salt and black pepper; set aside. In separate containers, set aside the flour, olive oil, onions, and garlic. If using shiitake or portobello mushrooms, cut off and discard the stems, then cut the mushrooms into ¼-inch-wide strips; if using chanterelle mushrooms, cut into ¼-inch-wide strips; if using morel mushrooms, cut the mushrooms in half lengthwise. Set aside the mushrooms. In a bowl, combine the pepper, tomato, and sausage. In a small fine-meshed sieve, rinse the rice until the rinse water is clear, then set aside to drain. In another bowl, combine the stock, Worcestershire sauce, chile sauce, bay leaves, basil, and thyme.

Place the chicken pieces on a baking sheet or a piece of waxed paper or parchment paper, lightly flour the pieces, then shake each piece to remove any excess flour. Place a heavy 12-inch frying pan over medium-high heat and heat the olive oil. Sauté the chicken until the pieces are golden on both sides, a total of about 8 minutes.

Remove the chicken from the pot. Return the pot to medium-low heat and add the onions. Sauté the onions until they are a light gold, about 8 minutes. Then add the mushrooms and garlic; sauté until the mushrooms soften slightly, about 8 minutes. Add the pepper, tomato, and sausage and sauté for 5 minutes. Stir in the rice. Place the chicken, skin side up, in the pot and add the chicken stock mixture. Bring to a low boil, cover the pan, reduce heat to simmer, and cook the chicken for 18 minutes.

Remove the chicken and let cool to room temperature, then cut the meat off the bones in large pieces. Discard the bones and skin. Cut the chicken meat into spoon-sized pieces. Return the chicken meat to the soup. *All advance preparation steps may be completed up to 8 hours before you begin the final cooking steps.*

FINAL COOKING STEPS

Bring the soup to a low simmer. Sprinkle half the filé powder over the soup and immediately stir it in. Simmer until the soup thickens, about 1 minute. Stir in the remaining filé powder to complete thickening (do not add if you prefer a thinner soup). Taste and adjust the seasoning, especially for salt. Transfer to a heated soup tureen or 4 heated soup bowls and serve at once.

SUGGESTED ACCOMPANIMENTS

Garlic-onion rolls, fennel salad, and chocolate-strawberry swirl bread pudding

Hot Chicken Perfection from the Grill and Barbecue

Grilling and barbecuing are the easiest ways to create complex-tasting chicken with a minimum of preparation time and only occasional supervision during cooking. Grilling and barbecuing sears and traps the chicken juices, browns and crisps the skin, concentrates and caramelizes the marinade, and infuses the chicken with unique smoky essences. The resulting layers of flavor make grilling and barbecuing the cooking method of choice for both everyday and festive chicken dinners.

Barbecuing means cooking over a gas, charcoal, or wood fire. *Grilling* means cooking the chicken on a flat cast-iron pan with a ridged surface. These rectangular pans are designed to be set over two burners. Because the ridges elevate the chicken, the underside of the meat does not steam and the marinade vaporizes. Grilling is an ideal way to cook boneless chicken breasts, with or without the skin, but does not work well for bone-in chicken pieces because the cooking time is too long and produces too much smoke. All the marinades in this chapter can be used interchangeably for both barbecuing and grilling.

To add an intense flavor to barbecued meat, soak 1 cup of wood chips in cold water for 30 minutes; drain and place the chips on a layer of aluminum foil positioned at one corner of the barbecue rack. When the wood begins to smoke, place the chicken on the barbecue and cover with the top.

Always barbecue chicken over medium heat. Place your open hand, palm-side down, 4 inches above the heat, and count "1001, 1002, 1003." The heat is medium if it's hot enough to make you pull your hand away at "1003." Turn the chicken several times during cooking, brushing on more of the marinade. Whenever you're not turning over the chicken, cover the barbecue so that the smoke is trapped inside. Because chicken breasts cook more quickly than the legs, when barbecuing chicken pieces, place the breasts on the barbecue 5 to 8 minutes after beginning to barbecue the thighs and drumsticks.

All of the recipes in this chapter also can be cooked in the oven. Roast chicken pieces with the bone in and the skin on, skin side up on a flat rack that rests on the edges of a roasting pan in a preheated 425-degree oven for approximately 30 minutes. Do not turn the pieces during roasting. Broil boneless chicken breasts in a preheated oven 4 inches from the heating element for approximately 3 minutes on each side.

The number of chicken-wing fanatics continues to grow. Chicken wings taste delicious because the meat has more fat than chicken breasts, and as all wing (and rib) devotees know, the meat closest to the bone tastes the sweetest. Always marinate chicken wings for a minimum of 8 hours or up to 24 hours so that the flavors permeate the meat. When barbecuing wings, medium to medium-low heat ensures long, slow cooking, which leads to crisp skin and extraordinarily tender meat. Any efforts to accelerate the cooking process will cause the marinade to burn.

Serves 4 to 8 as an appetizer, 2 to 4 as an entrée

Szechwan Barbecued Chicken Wings

INGREDIENTS

4 pounds chicken wings
1 orange for garnish

SZECHWAN BARBECUE SAUCE

½ cup freshly squeezed orange juice
⅔ cup hoisin sauce
¼ cup oyster sauce
¼ cup red wine vinegar
¼ cup honey
1 tablespoon dark sesame oil
1 tablespoon Asian chile sauce
2 tablespoons very finely minced ginger
6 cloves garlic, finely minced
½ cup minced whole green onions
1 tablespoon minced orange zest

ADVANCE PREPARATION
Rinse chicken wings with cold water, then pat dry. Cut off and discard the wing tips. In a large bowl, combine the barbecue sauce ingredients and mix thoroughly. Add the wings and mix to coat evenly. Cover and refrigerate for 8 to 24 hours, turning the wings 2 or 3 times. *All advance preparation steps may be completed up to 8 to 24 hours before you begin the final cooking steps.*

FINAL COOKING STEPS
Prepare the garnish by cutting the orange into ⅛-inch slices. Make a cut from the center to the edge of each slice; twist the slice and set aside to use as a garnish.

If using a gas barbecue, preheat to medium (350 degrees). If using charcoal or wood, prepare a fire. When the gas barbecue is hot or the coals or wood is ash covered, brush the cooking rack with oil, then lay the wings on the central, hottest part of the rack. Cover the barbecue. Barbecue the wings for about 30 to 40 minutes, turning them over every 10 minutes and brushing on more of the marinade. The wings are done when the skin turns a mahogany color. Serve at once.

If cooking the wings in the oven, preheat the oven to 375 degrees. Line a shallow baking pan with aluminum foil, spray a nonstick wire rack with a vegetable-oil cooking spray, and place the rack on the foil. Place the wings on the rack and roast for 1 hour. After the first 30 minutes of roasting, brush the wings with more marinade, turn the wings over, brush on more of the marinade, and roast another 30 minutes. Transfer the wings to a heated serving platter, garnish with the orange twists, and serve at once.

SUGGESTED ACCOMPANIMENTS
Caesar salad with chile croutons and peach cobbler with praline topping

This recipe uses chiles whose availability has spread from Mexican markets to American supermarkets. The lingering, mildly spicy, and sweet fruity flavor of dried ancho chiles adds a captivating element to barbecue sauces. The ancho is a dried poblano, which is a squat, purplish red crinkled chile, often mislabeled as "pasilla chile." Chipotle chiles in adobo sauce are smoked, dried jalapeños sold canned in a sauce made with tomatoes, vinegar, and garlic. Even small amounts of chipotle chiles in adobo sauce contribute a deeply smoky flavor and searing heat to food.

Cowboy Chicken with Ancho Chile Rub

Serves 4 as an entrée

INGREDIENTS

2 frying chickens, cut into pieces

3 ounces dried ancho chiles

¼ cup chipotle chiles in adobo sauce

3 tablespoons olive oil

2 tablespoons red wine vinegar

2 tablespoons thin soy sauce

2 tablespoons honey

1 small shallot, minced

8 cloves garlic, finely minced

¼ cup finely chopped cilantro

ADVANCE PREPARATION

Rinse the chickens with cold water, pat dry, and transfer to a mixing bowl. Seed and stem the ancho chiles. Bring 4 cups water to a boil in a medium saucepan. As soon as the water boils, turn off the heat, add the ancho chiles, and cover the saucepan. Soak the chiles for 30 minutes, stirring them occasionally. Discard the water.

Place the ancho chiles and chipotle chiles in a food processor. Blend until thoroughly puréed. Add all the remaining ingredients except the cilantro. Blend again to mix evenly. Pour the ancho chile rub onto the chicken, add the cilantro, and rub the chicken pieces until they are evenly coated with the marinade. Cover and refrigerate for at least 15 minutes but not longer than 8 hours. *All advance preparation may be completed up to 8 hours before you begin the final cooking steps.*

FINAL COOKING STEPS

If using a gas barbecue, preheat to medium (350 degrees). If using charcoal or wood, prepare a fire. When the gas barbecue is preheated or the coals or wood is ash covered, brush the cooking rack with oil, then lay the chicken, skin side up, in the center of the grill. Cover the barbecue. Regulate the heat so that it remains at a medium temperature. Barbecue the chicken about 12 minutes on each side. The chicken is done when an instant-read meat thermometer registers 170 degrees when inserted deeply into a thigh and the juices run clear when the chicken is pierced with a fork. As the chicken cooks, brush on any remaining ancho chile rub.

Alternatively, roast the chicken on a flat rack resting on the edges of a roasting pan in a preheated 425-degree oven. The chicken is done when it reaches an internal temperature of 170 degrees and the juices run clear, about 30 minutes. Transfer to a heated serving platter or 4 heated dinner plates and serve at once.

SUGGESTED ACCOMPANIMENTS

Fresh corn with garlic butter, vine-ripened tomato and basil salad, and strawberry pie

Chicken Storage and Safety

- Chicken is highly perishable. Always check the "sell by" date on the package label. This indicates the last day the product should be offered for sale, although it will maintain its high quality if properly refrigerated and cooked within 2 days of that date. Do not freeze chicken after the "sell by" date has passed. Use uncooked chicken within 2 days, and whole cooked chicken within 3 days.

- Plan to go directly home when buying chicken, and refrigerate the chicken immediately. Never leave chicken in your car for more than 1 hour, unless it is in an ice chest.

- If freezing chicken, wrap it airtight. Because the flavor and texture of chicken deteriorates the longer it is frozen, use whole chickens within 6 months and chicken parts within 3 months. Thaw chicken in the refrigerator or in cold water, but never at room temperature, which promotes bacterial growth. It takes approximately 24 hours to thaw a 4-pound chicken in the refrigerator, and 3 to 9 hours for chicken pieces. Alternatively, submerge the chicken in its original wrap or a water-tight plastic bag in cold water, change the water often. Chicken parts will take about 2 hours to defrost. For quick thawing, use the microwave. Select the defrost or medium-low setting, microwave the chicken for 2 minutes, turn the chicken or separate the chicken pieces, and continue microwaving and turning the chicken until it feels soft but is still cold. Once defrosted, never refreeze chicken.

- Always discard raw chicken if there is any odor (washing chicken that has begun to spoil will never make it safe to eat). After handling chicken, always wash your hands, countertops, cutting boards, knives, and other objects that have come into contact with the raw chicken for at least 20 seconds in hot soapy water. If you complete the preparation steps for a chicken recipe more than 15 minutes before cooking the chicken, always return the chicken to the refrigerator. And once the chicken has been cooked, always place it on a clean plate rather than on the same plate it rested on when raw.

- Handle marinades safely. Don't brush a marinade over chicken that is within 5 minutes of being removed from the barbecue or oven. If you want to spoon a marinade over cooked chicken, either set aside a portion of marinade that has never come into contact with the raw chicken, or boil the marinade for 30 seconds just before spooning it over the chicken. Once cooked chicken has cooled to room temperature, refrigerate it immediately. Cooked chicken should otherwise be kept at a temperature between 140 and 165 degrees. To reheat leftovers, cover the pan to retain moisture and to ensure that the chicken is heated all the way through, and bring any sauce surrounding the chicken to a rolling boil for 15 seconds.

- There has been much mention recently about the dangers of salmonella poisoning caused by eating chicken. Salmonella is an invisible, odorless bacteria that is widely prevalent in the environment. Any salmonella on chicken is destroyed when the internal temperature of chicken reaches 140 degrees. As long as you wash all implements, cutting boards, and your hands with hot soapy water and properly cook the chicken, there is no danger of salmonella poisoning.

Hot Chicken Facts

This is the first of several recipes scattered throughout this book that use the chicken skin as a pocket to trap a marinade against the surface of the breast, thigh, and leg meat. This is a great technique for adding maximum flavor to chicken. Either choose small chickens weighing 2 1/2 pounds each, so that each person is served half a chicken, or cut larger chicken halves into pieces after barbecuing. Because the breasts cook more quickly than the legs, cook the legs over the hottest part of the barbecue.

Serves 4 as an entrée

Thai Barbecued Chicken

INGREDIENTS

2 frying chickens, split in half

1/4 cup Chinese rice wine or dry sherry

1/4 cup oyster sauce

1/4 cup honey

2 tablespoons Asian chile sauce

Zest of 1 lime, finely minced

1/4 cup freshly squeezed lime juice

8 cloves garlic, finely minced

1/3 cup chopped cilantro

1/3 cup finely minced whole green onions

ADVANCE PREPARATION

Rinse the chicken with cold water, then pat dry. Working with 1 chicken half, loosen a small area of the skin along the top of the breast. Gently push your index finger underneath the skin, moving it along the breast, thigh, and drumstick, being careful not to dislodge the skin attached to the backbone. Repeat with the remaining chicken halves.

In a small bowl, combine all the remaining ingredients. Spoon 3 to 4 tablespoons of the marinade under the skin of one chicken half and, with your fingers, massage the outside of the skin to work the marinade over the breast, thigh, and drumstick. Repeat with the rest of the chicken halves. Rub remaining marinade over chicken. Place in a bowl, cover, and refrigerate for at least 30 minutes but not longer than 8 hours. *All advance preparation may be completed up to 8 hours before you begin the final cooking steps.*

FINAL COOKING STEPS

If using a gas barbecue, preheat it to medium (350 degrees). If using charcoal or wood, prepare a fire. When the gas barbecue is heated or the coals or wood is ash covered, brush the cooking rack with oil, then lay the chicken, skin side up, in the center of the rack. Cover the barbecue. Regulate the heat so that it remains at a medium temperature. Barbecue the chicken about 12 minutes on each side. The chicken is done when an instant-read meat thermometer registers 170 degrees when inserted deeply into a thigh and the juices run clear when the chicken is pierced with a fork. As the chicken cooks, brush on the remaining marinade.

Alternatively, place the chicken on a flat rack resting on the edges of a roasting pan in a preheated 425-degree oven. Cook until the internal temperature of the chicken reaches 170 degrees and the juices run clear, about 30 minutes.

Remove the chicken from the grill or oven and cut into pieces. Place the chicken on a heated platter or 4 heated dinner plates and serve at once.

SUGGESTED ACCOMPANIMENTS

Rice pilaf with red peppers and green onions; cucumber and rice vinegar salad; and coconut-raspberry ice cream

Middle Eastern Barbecued Chicken

I N G R E D I E N T S

2 frying chickens, cut into pieces

Zest from 2 lemons, finely minced

¾ cup freshly squeezed lemon juice

¾ cup olive oil

⅓ cup honey

1 tablespoon ground cumin

1 tablespoon sweet paprika

1 to 2 teaspoons cayenne

1½ teaspoons salt

6 cloves garlic, finely minced

4 small shallots, minced

½ cup chopped cilantro

½ cup chopped mint leaves

1 whole nutmeg

We use a special "tasting" vocabulary to better analyze the flavor of food. For example, this Middle Eastern-inspired barbecue dish has lingering deep "low notes" achieved from the cumin, garlic, and the smoky barbecue cooking process. Chicken provides the "middle notes" or a neutral stage upon which all the other flavors play their roles. "High notes," or sparkling bursts of flavor, come from lemon, paprika, cayenne, cilantro, mint, and freshly grated nutmeg. The dish acquires a "rounded" flavor or richness from the olive oil and honey, which help all the other flavors linger on the palate. "Depth of flavor" or the ability to intensify all the flavors is provided by the salt. Lastly, "good flavor balance" means all of the flavor elements create a harmonious, alluring taste sensation.

Serves 4 as an entrée

ADVANCE PREPARATION

Rinse the chicken with cold water, pat dry, and transfer to a mixing bowl. In a small bowl, combine all the remaining ingredients except the nutmeg. Stir thoroughly to combine. Pour the marinade over the chicken and rub the chicken pieces until they are evenly coated with the marinade. Cover and refrigerate for at least 15 minutes but not longer than 8 hours. *All advance preparation may be completed up to 8 hours before you begin the final cooking steps.*

FINAL COOKING STEPS

If using a gas barbecue, preheat to medium (350 degrees). If using charcoal or wood, prepare a fire. When the gas barbecue is heated or the coals or wood is ash covered, brush the cooking rack with oil, then lay the chicken, skin side up, on the rack. Cover the barbecue. Regulate the heat so that it remains at a medium temperature. Grill the chicken about 12 minutes on each side. As the chicken cooks, brush on any remaining marinade. The chicken is done when an instant-read meat thermometer registers 170 degrees when inserted deeply into a thigh and the juices will run clear when the chicken is pierced with a fork. Transfer to a serving platter or 4 heated dinner plates. Using a nutmeg grater or cheese grater, add a small dusting of fresh nutmeg across the top of the pieces.

Alternatively, place the chicken on a flat rack resting on the edges of a roasting pan in a preheated 425-degree oven. Cook until the internal temperature reaches 170 degrees and the juices run clear, about 25 minutes. Dust with freshly grated nutmeg and serve at once.

SUGGESTED ACCOMPANIMENTS

Tabbouleh with parsley and pine nuts, hot garlic eggplant, and lemon tart

Sizzling Rosemary-Mustard Chicken

The wait is worth the taste: Chicken breasts with the bones and skin attached take longer to cook than either boned or boned and skinned breasts, but the taste is far superior. The breastbones distribute the heat and, along with the skin, provide a protective shield that keeps the meat tender when exposed to the barbecue heat. Elsewhere in this chapter, a marinade is rubbed under the skin of chicken halves. Don't use this technique when barbecuing chicken breasts, because the loosened skin will shift off the meat as you turn the chicken during barbecuing.

Serves 4 as an entrée

INGREDIENTS

8 chicken breast halves, bone in and skin on
¼ cup finely chopped fresh rosemary
5 cloves garlic, finely minced
2 shallots, minced
10 juniper berries, ground in a mortar
1 tablespoon minced lemon zest
½ cup dry vermouth
⅓ cup freshly squeezed lemon juice
⅓ cup extra virgin olive oil
⅓ cup Dijon mustard
⅓ cup thin soy sauce
¼ cup honey
2 teaspoons Asian chile sauce

ADVANCE PREPARATION

Rinse the chicken with cold water, then pat dry. Using a heavy knife or poultry shears, trim away any exposed rib bone ends and cut away the wing sockets. In a large bowl, combine all the remaining ingredients. Stir well to evenly mix, then add the chicken. Turn the chicken in the marinade until it is evenly coated. Cover and refrigerate for at least 30 minutes but not longer than 8 hours. *All advance preparation may be completed up to 8 hours before you begin the final cooking steps.*

FINAL COOKING STEPS

If using a gas barbecue, preheat to medium (350 degrees). If using charcoal or wood, prepare a fire. When the gas barbecue is heated or the coals or wood is ash covered, brush the cooking rack with oil, then lay the chicken, skin side up, on the rack. Cover the barbecue. Regulate the heat so that it remains at a medium temperature. Grill the chicken about 8 minutes on each side. As the chicken cooks, intermittently brush on the remaining marinade. The chicken is done when an instant-read meat thermometer registers 160 degrees when inserted deeply into the breast and the juices run clear when the chicken is pierced with a fork.

Alternatively, place the chicken on a flat rack resting on the edges of a roasting pan in a preheated 425-degree oven. Cook until the internal temperature reaches 160 degrees and the juices run clear, about 30 minutes. Transfer to a heated platter or 4 heated dinner plates and serve at once.

SUGGESTED ACCOMPANIMENTS

Spicy stuffed mushrooms, zucchini and tomato ratatouille, and date-nut cake

*F*ruit and chicken have a special affinity for each other. In this recipe, raspberries, red wine, cumin, and chiles are boiled to concentrate their flavor, then strained twice to remove all the seeds. This can be completed a day ahead. When the sauce is reheated during the final moments of simmering, unsalted butter is stirred into it, which contributes a rich taste and causes all the flavors to linger on the palate. Even if fresh raspberries are not in season, the intense raspberry flavor will be identical when using the less-expensive frozen unsweetened raspberries sold year-round by every supermarket.

Raspberry Cabernet Chicken

Serves 4 as an entrée

INGREDIENTS

6 to 8 chicken breast halves, boned but skin on

¼ cup dry vermouth

2 tablespoons oyster sauce

2 tablespoons light olive oil

½ teaspoon freshly ground black pepper

RASPBERRY-CABERNET SAUCE

2 cloves garlic, finely minced

2 tablespoons very finely minced ginger

2 tablespoons cooking oil

12 ounces frozen unsweetened raspberries

2 cups dry red wine

¼ cup sugar

½ teaspoon Asian chile sauce

½ teaspoon salt

¼ teaspoon ground cumin

2 tablespoons unsalted butter

¼ cup sour cream (optional)

¼ cup chopped fresh chives

½ pint fresh raspberries

ADVANCE PREPARATION

Rinse the chicken with cold water, then pat dry. Combine the vermouth, oyster sauce, olive oil, and pepper. Rub the mixture over chicken to coat evenly. Cover and refrigerate for at least 15 minutes but not longer than 8 hours.

To make the sauce, place a nonreactive 12-inch skillet or sauté pan over medium-high heat. Add the garlic, ginger, and cooking oil. Sauté the garlic until it begins to sizzle but does not brown. Add the raspberries, wine, sugar, chile sauce, salt, and cumin. Turn the heat to high, bring the sauce to a rapid boil, and boil to reduce to 1¾ cups. Immediately pour the sauce into a medium-meshed sieve placed over a bowl. Using a metal spoon, scrape the sieve, forcing all the pulp through but leaving most of the seeds behind. Scrape off and add to the bowl the raspberry pulp clinging to the underside of the sieve. Strain the raspberry sauce a second time to remove all seeds.

In separate containers, cover and set aside the butter, sour cream, chives, and fresh raspberries. *All advance preparation may be completed up to 8 hours before you begin the final cooking steps.*

FINAL COOKING STEPS

If using a gas barbecue, preheat to medium (350 degrees). If using charcoal or wood, prepare a fire. When the gas barbecue is heated or the coals or wood is ash covered, brush the cooking rack with oil, then lay the chicken, skin side down, on the rack. Regulate the heat so that it remains at a medium temperature. Barbecue the chicken about 5 minutes on each side. As the chicken cooks, brush on any remaining marinade. The chicken is done when an instant-read meat thermometer registers 150 degrees when inserted deeply into a breast and the juices run clear when the chicken is pierced with a fork. Temporarily transfer the chicken to a plate.

Alternatively, place the chicken on a rack 4 inches below the heating element of a preheated broiler, and broil the chicken skin side up until the internal heat reaches 150 degrees and the juices run clear, about 8 minutes. If the skin becomes crisp, but the breasts are not fully cooked, turn the chicken over.

In a small nonreactive saucepan, bring the raspberry cabernet sauce to a low boil. Remove the pan from the heat and stir in the butter. Pour the sauce across the surface of 4 heated dinner plates. Place 1 or 2 pieces of chicken in the center of each plate or slice the chicken and place the slices on each plate. Decorate the sauce with little dots of sour cream, sprinkle the chives over, garnish with the fresh raspberries and serve at once.

SUGGESTED ACCOMPANIMENTS

Wild rice pilaf, East-West asparagus salad, and praline peach pie

East-West Grilled Teriyaki Chicken

Teriyaki ("shining broil") refers to the dark, glossy sheen that teriyaki sauce contributes when brushed across chicken, seafood, or vegetables. For this recipe, equal amounts of mirin (sake sweetened with sugar), sake, and dark soy sauce serve as the foundation for the marinade, accented by the subtle anise flavor of minced fresh basil leaves. Part of the mixture is reduced to concentrate its flavor, then it is slightly thickened with cornstarch before a little butter is added during the final moments of cooking to add a rich "mouth feel." For a variation, substitute skin-on chicken breasts for the chicken thighs.

Serves 4 as an entrée

INGREDIENTS

¾ cup mirin

¾ cup sake

¾ cup dark soy sauce

3 tablespoons sugar

3 tablespoons very finely minced ginger

2 tablespoons minced basil leaves

10 chicken thighs

½ fresh pineapple, peeled, cored, and cut into ¼-inch-thick slices

8 whole green onions

12 shiitake mushrooms, stemmed

2 medium tomatoes, sliced

2 teaspoons cornstarch

2 tablespoons unsalted butter

ADVANCE PREPARATION

In a small saucepan, combine the mirin, sake, soy, sugar, ginger, and basil. Bring to a boil, then, in a bowl that is large enough to hold the chicken, set aside ¾ cup of the liquid to use as the chicken marinade, and cool to room temperature. In a small bowl, set aside another ¾ cup of the remaining liquid to use as the vegetable marinade. In a small saucepan over high heat, boil the remaining liquid until it is reduced to ½ cup to make a teriyaki sauce; set aside.

Rinse the chicken with cold water, then pat dry. Trim all excess fat from around the edges of the thighs. Transfer the thighs to the bowl holding the chicken marinade, and turn to coat them evenly. Cover and refrigerate the chicken for at least 15 minutes, but not longer than 8 hours. In separate covered containers, refrigerate the pineapple, green onions, mushrooms, and tomatoes. *All advance preparations may be completed up to 8 hours before you begin the final cooking steps.*

FINAL COOKING STEPS

Combine the cornstarch with an equal amount of cold water. Set aside the butter. If using a gas barbecue, preheat it to medium (350 degrees). If using charcoal or wood, prepare a fire. When the gas barbecue is preheated or the coals or wood is ash covered, brush the cooking rack with oil, then lay the chicken, skin side up, in the center of the rack. Cover the barbecue. Barbecue the chicken about 14 minutes on each side. The chicken is done when an instant-read meat thermometer registers 170 degrees when inserted deeply into a thigh and the juices run clear when the chicken is pierced with a fork. Brush the chicken marinade on the chicken as it cooks. During the last 8 minutes of cooking, place the pineapple, green onions, mushrooms, and tomatoes on the grill. Brush the vegetables with the vegetable marinade. The vegetables are done when they acquire grill marks on all sides, and the mushrooms soften slightly, about 8 minutes.

Alternatively, place the chicken and vegetables on a flat rack resting on the edges of a roasting pan in a preheated 425-degree oven. Cook the chicken until an instant-read meat thermometer registers 170 degrees and the juices run clear, about 30 minutes.

Transfer the chicken, pineapple, green onions, mushrooms, and tomatoes to a heated serving platter or 4 heated dinner plates. Bring the teriyaki sauce to a low boil, then stir the cornstarch mixture into the sauce. Return the sauce to a low boil, remove the saucepan from the heat, and stir the butter into the sauce until it is incorporated. Brush the teriyaki sauce over the chicken, fruit, and vegetables. Serve at once.

SUGGESTED ACCOMPANIMENTS

Steamed jasmine rice and ginger crème brûlée

Grilled Five-Spice Chicken with Apples

Five-spice powder, a blend of star anise, fennel seeds, cinnamon, Szechwan pepper, and cloves, is sold in 1-ounce bags in Asian markets and in the spice section of virtually all supermarkets. Five-spice powder contributes an exotic, complex flavor to chicken marinades and sauces, but because it is strong, only small amounts are used. In this recipe, the marinade of five-spice powder, chiles, plum sauce, and the sweetened Japanese sake called mirin, is a perfect flavor marriage with boneless skin-on chicken breasts and crisp apples, such as Fujis or Braeburns.

Serves 4 as an entrée

INGREDIENTS

6 to 8 chicken breast halves, boned but skin on

2 Fuji or other crisp apples

¾ cup mirin

5 tablespoons hoisin sauce

3 tablespoons oyster sauce

3 tablespoons plum sauce

3 tablespoons thin soy sauce

1½ teaspoons five-spice powder

1½ teaspoons Asian chile sauce

3 cloves garlic, finely minced

2 tablespoons very finely minced ginger

2 whole green onions, minced

1 bunch fresh chives

ADVANCE PREPARATION

Rinse the chicken with cold water, then pat dry. Quarter and core (but do not peel) the apples. Combine all the remaining ingredients except the chives. In a bowl, combine the apples with ½ cup of the marinade, mix well, and refrigerate. In another bowl, combine the chicken with the remaining marinade. Mix well to coat evenly. Cover and refrigerate for at least 15 minutes but not longer than 8 hours. *All advance preparation may be completed up to 8 hours before you begin the final cooking steps.*

FINAL COOKING STEPS

Finely chop the chives and set aside. Follow the instructions for barbecuing the chicken, or alternatively place a grill pan over 2 burners turned to medium. When the grill pan becomes very hot, spray it with vegetable-oil cooking spray or rub it with cooking oil, and place the chicken, skin side down, in the pan. Grill the chicken breasts for approximately 2 minutes on each side, brushing on more marinade during cooking. The chicken is done as soon as it feels firm to the touch and has reached an internal temperature of 150 degrees. As the chicken cooks, add the apples and cook them on both sides until they are hot in the center, about 5 minutes. Do not brush any of the chicken marinade on the apples.

If using a gas barbecue, preheat to medium (350 degrees). If using charcoal or wood, prepare a fire. When the gas barbecue is heated or the coals or wood is ash covered, brush the cooking rack with oil, then lay the chicken, skin side down, in the center of the rack. Barbecue the chicken until it feels firm to the touch, about 2 minutes on each side, brushing on more marinade during cooking. The chicken is done when it reaches an internal temperature of 150 degrees and the juices run clear. Grill the apples next to the chicken, cooking the apples on both sides until well heated, about 5 minutes. Again, do not brush any of the chicken marinade on the apples.

Alternatively, place the chicken, skin side up, on a rack and place 4 inches below the heating element of a preheated broiler. Broil the chicken until it reaches an internal temperature of 150 degrees and the juices run clear, about 8 minutes. If the skin becomes crisp but the breasts are not done, turn the chicken over.

Transfer the chicken and apples to a heated serving platter or 4 heated dinner plates, sprinkle on the chives, and serve at once.

SUGGESTED ACCOMPANIMENTS

Watercress salad, fireworks rice pilaf, and chocolate chip almond cookies

Tandoori Chicken with Cilantro-Mint Sauce

Atandoor is a clay oven, open at the top, with a charcoal or wood fire inside. Originally from Central Asia, these ovens have long been popular in northwest India. Tandoori chicken is marinated with yogurt and a spice blend called **garam masala** which, with the addition of cooking oil, becomes a curry paste. In India, a natural dye called **tandoori rang** is added to color the meat red, or you can add paprika. Although the chicken is traditionally skinned and the meat is slashed to help the marinade permeate to the bone, we like to barbecue the chicken with the marinade under the skin.

Serves 4 as an entrée

INGREDIENTS

2 frying chickens, split in half

1 cup plain yogurt

¼ cup freshly squeezed lemon juice

INDIAN CURRY PASTE

6 cloves garlic

1-inch length ginger, thinly sliced

4 dried red chiles, seeded

1 teaspoon black peppercorns

1 teaspoon cumin seeds

1 teaspoon coriander seeds

½ teaspoon mustard seeds

Seeds from 6 cardamom pods

1 clove

½-inch stick cinnamon

1 teaspoon salt

1 teaspoon ground turmeric

½ teaspoon freshly grated nutmeg

¼ teaspoon ground mace

¼ cup cooking oil

CILANTRO-MINT SAUCE

½ cup tightly packed cilantro sprigs

¼ cup mint leaves

¼ cup water

2 tablespoons plain yogurt

2 teaspoons freshly squeezed lemon juice

½ teaspoon salt

½ teaspoon ground cumin

ADVANCE PREPARATION

Rinse the chicken with cold water, then pat dry. Working with one chicken half, loosen a small area of the skin along the top of the breast, then loosen the skin along the breast, thigh, and drumstick. Repeat with the remaining chicken halves. Combine the yogurt and lemon juice, and set aside.

To make the Indian Curry Paste, in a blender or food processor, mince the garlic and ginger. In a small skillet or sauté pan, combine the chiles, peppercorns, cumin, coriander, mustard, cardamom, clove, and cinnamon. Sauté over medium heat until the mustard seeds begin to pop, about 2 minutes. Using a spice grinder, grind the spices into a powder. Transfer the powder to the food processor bowl containing the garlic and ginger, and add the salt, turmeric, nutmeg, and mace. With the motor running, slowly add the cooking oil, and process into a paste. (Makes ⅓ cup paste that can be stored for up to 6 months in the refrigerator.)

Transfer the curry paste to a small bowl and add the yogurt and lemon juice. Stir to evenly combine. Spoon the marinade under the chicken skin, working it across the breast and leg meat. Rub the remaining marinade on the outside of the chicken pieces. Place in a bowl, cover, and refrigerate for 8 to 24 hours.

To make the Cilantro-Mint Sauce, mince the cilantro and mint in an electric mini-chopper, add the remaining ingredients and process until evenly mixed. Cover and refrigerate. *All advance preparation may be completed up to 8 to 24 hours before you begin the final cooking steps.*

FINAL COOKING STEPS

If using a gas barbecue, preheat to medium (350 degrees). If using charcoal or wood, prepare a fire. When the gas barbecue is heated or the coals or wood is ash covered, brush the cooking rack with oil, then lay the chicken skin side up on the rack. Grill the chicken for about 12 minutes on each side. The chicken is done when an instant-read meat thermometer registers 170 degrees when plunged deeply into a thigh and the juices run clear when the chicken is pierced with a fork. As the chicken cooks, brush on remaining marinade.

Alternatively, place the chicken on a flat rack resting on the edges of a roasting pan in a 425-degree oven. Cook until the internal temperature reaches 170 degrees and the juices run clear, about 30 minutes.

Remove the chicken from the barbecue and cut it into pieces. Place the chicken on a heated platter or 4 heated dinner plates and serve with the Mint-Cilantro Sauce.

SUGGESTED ACCOMPANIMENTS

Yogurt and cucumber raita, lentil dal, and honey and pecan peach ice cream

Jerk Chicken with Pineapple Salsa

**J**erk is a Jamaican marinade of allspice, nutmeg, cinnamon, fresh chiles, and other seasonings that is rubbed on pork or chicken before it is cooked in a pit covered by green allspice branches. Jerk supposedly originated over 300 years ago as a marinating and cooking method of the Maroons, a group of escaped African slaves. According to legend, Lady Nugent, the wife of one of the island's British governors, tasted jerk and liked it so much that she popularized this dish. The unique flavors of jerk marinade are great when rubbed across a butterflied leg of lamb or on jumbo prawns to be barbecued.

Serves 4 to 10 as an appetizer, 2 as an entrée

INGREDIENTS

16 4-inch-long bamboo skewers

6 chicken thighs, boned but skin on

JERK SAUCE

2 dried ancho chiles

2 shallots

½-inch length ginger, thinly sliced

4 cloves garlic

4 serrano or Thai chiles, stemmed and finely minced, including seeds, plus additional whole chiles for garnish

2 tablespoons minced fresh mint leaves

¼ cup cooking oil

¼ cup thin soy sauce

2 tablespoons honey

2 tablespoons freshly squeezed lime juice

1 teaspoon ground allspice

1 teaspoon salt

1 teaspoon freshly ground black pepper

½ teaspoon ground cloves

½ teaspoon freshly ground nutmeg

PINEAPPLE SALSA

½ fresh ripe pineapple, peeled and cored

⅓ cup chopped cilantro sprigs

1 tablespoon very finely minced ginger

2 tablespoons freshly squeezed orange juice

2 tablespoons packed light brown sugar

½ teaspoon Asian or Caribbean chile sauce

1 sprig cilantro

ADVANCE PREPARATION

Cover the skewers with hot water and soak for 1 to 24 hours. Rinse the chicken with cold water, then pat dry. Cut each thigh into 3 strips. Place 1 piece of chicken on a cutting board, put the fingers of one hand on the chicken to stabilize it and, with the other hand, push the skewer down the length of the strip. The skewer should be visible only at either end of the chicken strip. Repeat with the remaining strips.

Seed and stem the ancho chiles. To make the Jerk Sauce, in a small saucepan, bring 4 cups of water to a boil, then remove from heat and add the ancho chiles. Cover the saucepan and soak the chiles for 30 minutes, stirring occasionally. Place the shallots, ginger, garlic, and serrano chiles in a food processor and mince finely. Add the ancho chile and process into a paste. Add the remaining jerk ingredients, and process into a smooth paste. (Makes ¾ cups Jerk Sauce; store in an airtight container in the refrigerator for up to 6 months.) Rub the Jerk Sauce over the chicken. Place in a container, cover, and refrigerate at least 15 minutes but no longer than 8 hours.

To make the salsa, chop the pineapple. Transfer the pineapple to a bowl, add the remaining salsa ingredients, and stir well. Cover and refrigerate. _All advance preparation may be completed up to 8 hours before you begin the final cooking steps._

FINAL COOKING STEPS

If using a gas barbecue, preheat to medium (350 degrees). If using charcoal or wood, prepare a fire. When the coals or wood is ash covered, brush the cooking rack with oil, then barbecue the chicken about 2 minutes on each side or until it has lost its raw interior color.

Alternatively, place the skewers on a flat rack resting on the edges of a roasting pan, cover the exposed bamboo ends with foil, and place the pan 4 inches below the heating element of a preheated broiler. Broil the skewers on both sides until the chicken has lost its raw interior color, about 3 minutes.

Transfer to a heated serving platter or 4 heated dinner plates. Chop the cilantro and sprinkle it over chicken. Serve at once accompanied with the Pineapple Salsa.

SUGGESTED ACCOMPANIMENTS

Couscous infused with mint, endive salad with tricolored peppers, and candy cane ice cream with fudge sauce

Hot Chicken Sizzling in Woks and Sauté Pans

Stir-frying and sautéing are techniques beloved by creative cooks. In these action-packed techniques, sizzling oil, changes in food color, and dramatic explosions of aroma determine the timing of the sequential, rhythmic cooking steps. The hot wok or hot sauté pan sears the chicken, sealing the juices inside and producing a rapid transfer of heat into the interior of the meat. Because these are last-minute techniques and because the limited heat source restricts the amount of food that can be successfully stir-fried or sautéed, serve these dishes to family and small groups of friends who may want to observe the action or offer a helping hand.

For stir-frying, all the sauces may be used interchangeably, other seasonal vegetables substituted, and the standard seasonings of garlic, chiles, and ginger varied. Use a heavy flat-bottomed 14- or 16-inch diameter wok with one long wooden handle and a second short handle, or a 14-inch cast-iron frying pan. Keep the heat high and never reduce the heat during the cooking process. Use boneless, skinless thigh or breast meat that is cut into very small pieces no thicker than ¼ inch. This ensures quick, even cooking. As soon as the chicken loses all of its raw color, it is fully cooked. Never stir-fry more than 1 pound of chicken in a wok at one time. If you increase the amount of chicken, have a friend stir-fry a second portion in a neighboring wok, duplicating your every move.

For sautéing, use a heavy 12- or 14-inch sauté pan. Preheat the pan until very hot before adding the cooking oil. This seals the surface of the pan so that the chicken will not stick. Whether using chicken cut into pieces, boneless skin-on chicken breasts, or skinned boneless chicken breasts, dust the chicken with flour, bread crumbs, or cornstarch. This prevents the chicken from splattering in the oil. Unlike the high heat used for stir-frying, the heat should be regulated so that the oil is always sizzling but is not smoking. For bone-in chicken, once the chicken has browned, add a sauce, cover the pan, and simmer the chicken until cooked. On the other hand, for boneless chicken breasts (with or without the skin), brown and then sauté the chicken until it is fully cooked, transfer it to a heated plate, and quickly make a sauce in the pan. The cooking steps are kept separate because simmering boneless chicken breasts with a sauce gives the meat a rubbery texture.

Be creative when sautéing chicken. Use any of the sauces in this chapter interchangeably or embark on your own culinary adventure by changing seasonings. Stir in the Tomato Cream Sauce from the Creole chicken recipe in lieu of the tangerine glaze when making Tangier Chicken. As the sauce reduces in the pan, sprinkle it with a different blend of finely chopped fresh herbs, stir in a big pinch of saffron threads to turn the sauce a brilliant yellow, or add pitted Mediterranean olives marinated with chiles for an assertive flavor impact.

The next time a stir-fry sauce lists chicken stock, rice wine, or coconut milk as its main ingredient, try substituting fresh citrus juice. In particular, the juice from tangerines and blood oranges, as well as the always available fresh juice from navel and Valencia oranges, makes an ideal foundation for Asian-style stir-fry sauces. The subtle citrus flavor marries well with simple combinations of rice wine and hoisin sauce, minced gingerroot, and dark sesame oil and, in this recipe, with more complex blends of Asian seasonings. Because the quality of fresh citrus juice deteriorates quickly, be sure to squeeze the juice fresh within hours of use.

Mongolian Chicken

Serves 4 as an entrée

INGREDIENTS

6 chicken thighs, boned and skinned

1 tablespoon hoisin sauce

1 tablespoon oyster sauce

1 tablespoon dark sesame oil

1 tablespoon Chinese rice wine or dry sherry

4 cloves garlic, finely minced

1/2 cup hazelnuts

14 medium button mushrooms

6 whole green onions

12 small dried red chiles

1/4 cup cooking oil

WOK SAUCE

1 teaspoon minced tangerine zest

1/3 cup freshly squeezed tangerine juice

1/4 cup Chinese rice wine or dry sherry

2 tablespoons oyster sauce

1 tablespoon hoisin sauce

1 tablespoon dark sesame oil

1 tablespoon red wine vinegar

1 tablespoon cornstarch

ADVANCE PREPARATION

Preheat the oven to 325 degrees (to toast the nuts). Rinse the chicken with cold water, then pat dry. Cut the meat lengthwise into 1/4-inch-wide strips. Cut the strips in half. In a small bowl, combine the chicken with the hoisin sauce, oyster sauce, sesame oil, rice wine, and garlic. Mix thoroughly to coat the chicken. Cover and refrigerate the chicken for at least 15 minutes but not longer than 8 hours.

Place the hazelnuts on a baking sheet and toast in the preheated oven for 15 minutes, or until the nuts become golden. If the papery skins are still on the nuts, wrap them in a kitchen towel and let cool for a few minutes. Rub the towel vigorously between your palms until all the skins have been removed. Set the nuts aside. Cut each mushroom through the stem into 4 wedges. Cut the green onions on a sharp diagonal into 1-inch lengths. Combine and set aside the green onions, mushrooms, and the dried chiles. Set aside the cooking oil. In a small bowl, combine the wok sauce ingredients and set aside. *All advance preparation may be completed up to 8 hours before you begin the final cooking steps.*

FINAL COOKING STEPS

Place a wok over the highest heat. When the wok is very hot, add half the cooking oil. Roll the oil around the wok to coat the inside, and when the oil gives off just a wisp of smoke, add the chicken. Stir and toss the chicken until it loses its raw exterior color, about 1 minute. Immediately transfer the chicken to a plate.

Immediately return the wok to the highest heat. Add the remaining cooking oil and, when the oil is hot, add the vegetables and chiles. Stir and toss the vegetables until the green onions brighten, about 2 minutes.

Stir the wok sauce, and pour it into the wok. Return the chicken to the wok, add the nuts, and stir and toss until all the ingredients are glazed with sauce. Taste and adjust the seasoning. Immediately transfer the stir-fry to a heated platter or 4 heated dinner plates and serve.

SUGGESTED ACCOMPANIMENTS

Pan-fried noodle nests and fresh strawberry shortcake

A sizzling hot wok sears chicken but keeps it tender, instantly brightens the colors of vegetables, and lets you quickly combine flavors that will entice your friends to the table. This recipe uses chicken thighs because their rich meat is a good match for the assertive flavors of coconut, chiles, and lime. Since boning and skinning chicken thighs is time-consuming, have your butcher complete this step for you. Whether using thighs or breasts for stir-fries, never cut the meat into pieces more than $1/4$ inch thick or it will not be cooked in the center after the brief amount of time it will be in the wok.

Serves 4 as an entrée

Thai Chicken Stir-Fry

INGREDIENTS

6 chicken thighs, boned and skinned
1 tablespoon oyster sauce
1 tablespoon dark sesame oil
1 tablespoon Chinese rice wine or dry sherry
2 medium green zucchini
2 medium yellow crookneck squash
4 whole green onions
$1/4$ cup cooking oil

WOK SEASONINGS

2 serrano chiles, finely minced (including the seeds)
4 cloves garlic, finely minced
1 tablespoon very finely minced ginger

WOK SAUCE

1 lime
$1/4$ cup chopped cilantro sprigs
$1/3$ cup Chinese rice wine or dry sherry
$1/3$ cup coconut milk
2 tablespoons Thai fish sauce
1 tablespoon oyster sauce
2 teaspoons cornstarch

ADVANCE PREPARATION

Rinse the chicken with cold water, then pat dry. Cut the meat lengthwise into $1/4$-inch-wide strips. Cut the strips into $3/4$-inch lengths. Place the chicken in a bowl and add the oyster sauce, sesame oil, and rice wine. Stir to evenly coat the chicken. Cover and refrigerate at least 15 minutes but not longer than 8 hours.

Cut the zucchini and squash in half lengthwise, then cut each piece in half lengthwise again. Place the strips together and cut across them to make $3/4$-inch lengths. Cut the green onions on a sharp diagonal to make 1-inch-long pieces. In a bowl, combine the zucchini, squash, and green onions, and set aside. Set aside the cooking oil. In a small bowl, combine the wok seasonings. To make the wok sauce, zest the lime and finely mince the zest. Place the zest in a small bowl. To the minced zest, add the remaining wok sauce ingredients. Stir well and set aside. Cut the lime in half and set aside. *All advance preparation may be completed up to 8 hours before you begin the final cooking steps.*

FINAL COOKING STEPS

Place a wok over the highest heat. When the wok becomes very hot, add half the cooking oil. Roll the oil around the wok to coat the inside, and when the oil gives off just a wisp of smoke, add the chicken. Stir and toss the chicken until it loses its raw exterior color, about 1 minute. Immediately transfer the chicken to a plate.

Immediately return the wok to the highest heat. Add the remaining cooking oil and the wok seasonings. Stir-fry for about 5 seconds, then add the vegetables. Stir and toss the vegetables until the green onions brighten in color, about 2 minutes.

Stir the wok sauce, then pour it into the wok. Return the chicken to the wok and stir and toss until all the ingredients are glazed with the sauce. Taste and adjust the seasoning, adding lime juice to taste. Immediately transfer the mixture to a heated platter or 4 heated dinner plates and serve.

SUGGESTED ACCOMPANIMENTS

Chilled shrimp with mango dressing, citrus rice pilaf, and bananas with Kahlúa sauce

- For serving amounts, count on 2 meaty pieces (breast halves, thighs, or legs) per person, whether the chicken is bone-in or boneless. Each pound of whole chicken will yield about 1 cup cooked chicken meat. Twelve ounces of skinned and boned chicken breasts will yield 2 cups of cooked chicken.

- The color of the skin gives no indication about the flavor of chicken. The yellow pigmentation of chicken skin is derived from xanthophyll, which occurs naturally in yellow corn. Chickens that are fed a high-corn diet have yellow skin, while chickens fed grains such as wheat, oats, or barley (which do not contain xanthophyll) will not have yellow skin.

- Rinsing chicken with cold water does not "clean" it or make it bacteria free. The purpose for rinsing chicken is just to wash away any chicken juices that may have accumulated around the chicken in the package.

- The taste and texture of fresh chicken is superior to that of frozen chicken. Freezing promotes the oxidation of fats, especially the unsaturated fats in chicken, and this eventually results in rancid flavors no matter how quickly the chicken was frozen. In addition, freezing chicken damages the tissue so that there is a loss of its nutrient-rich juices.

- Tests have proven that the fat content of chicken meat cooked with and without the skin is identical. Since the skin shields the meat from drying heat and keeps the meat tender during cooking, chicken should be cooked with its skin on. We always serve chicken with the skin attached and let our guests decide whether to remove it.

- Unfortunately, packaged bone-in chicken breasts often vary drastically in size within the same package. To guarantee that bone-in chicken breasts are the same size, buy unpackaged chicken breasts.

- Marinate chicken in the refrigerator for a minimum of 15 minutes and no longer than 8 hours. Longer marinating extracts moisture from the meat, breaks down the meat fibers, and results in less intensely chicken-flavored meat.

- Use vinaigrette as a foundation for flavor-intense marinades, then add finely chopped fresh herbs and aromatics such as minced garlic and ginger. If you include citrus juice, use the marinade that day, because the flavor of citrus deteriorates quickly.

- For added flavor impact when using oil- and fruit juice-based marinades, make an extra amount of marinade, keep it separate from the raw chicken, and once the cooked chicken is transferred to dinner plates, spoon the reserved marinade over the chicken.

- Never stuff a chicken until just before roasting it, because bacterial growth might occur. However, stuffing can be made hours ahead and refrigerated. Since the stuffing expands during roasting, remember to stuff the chicken only three-fourths full so that the chicken doesn't "pop."

- When sautéing boneless chicken breasts, use an equal amount of butter and oil. Butter, which contains milk solids, browns during cooking, giving the chicken a richer color and more intense flavor.

Hot Chicken Preparation Tips

Chicken Dancing with Mushrooms

The exciting element for all the chicken stir-fry recipes in this book is that all the sauces, vegetable combinations, and the use of thigh and breast meat are interchangeable from recipe to recipe. Whole preparation stages can even be eliminated! One night stir-fry the seasonings, such as ginger and garlic, then add the chicken, and when it is nearly cooked, stir in the sauce for a final few moments of cooking. Rolled inside hot flour or corn tortillas and accompanied with a simple dinner salad, this is an easy and healthful dinner after a busy workday. Or create your own chicken marinade, stir-fry the marinated chicken, and then slide it into a soup or toss it with a dinner salad.

Serves 4 as an entrée

INGREDIENTS

4 chicken breast halves, boned and skinned

1 tablespoon Chinese rice wine or dry sherry

1 tablespoon oyster sauce

1 tablespoon dark sesame oil

8 ounces firm fresh mushrooms (button, shiitakes, portobellos, or chanterelles)

12 stalks asparagus

3 whole green onions

¼ cup pine nuts

3 cloves garlic, finely minced

¼ cup cooking oil

¼ cup water

WOK SAUCE

¼ cup chicken stock

¼ cup Chinese rice wine or dry sherry

2 tablespoons oyster sauce

1 tablespoon dark sesame oil

1 tablespoon cornstarch

1 teaspoon sugar

¼ teaspoon freshly ground black pepper

ADVANCE PREPARATION

Rinse the chicken with cold water, then pat dry. Cut each breast lengthwise into ¼-inch-wide strips. Place the strips together and cut across them to make 1-inch-long pieces. Transfer the chicken to a small bowl and add the rice wine, oyster sauce, and sesame oil. Mix thoroughly, then cover and refrigerate for at least 15 minutes but not longer than 8 hours.

Preheat the oven to 325 degrees (to toast the nuts). Cut the button mushrooms into ¼-inch-thick slices; if using shiitake or portobello mushrooms, cut off and discard the stems, then cut the caps into thin wedges. Snap off and discard the tough asparagus ends. Cut the asparagus on a sharp diagonal, rotating the asparagus one quarter turn toward you after each cut. Cut the green onions on a sharp diagonal into 1-inch lengths. Combine the vegetables, cover, and refrigerate. Place the pine nuts on a baking sheet and toast in the preheated oven until they turn golden, about 8 minutes, then set aside. In separate containers, set aside the garlic, cooking oil, and water. In a small bowl, combine the ingredients for the wok sauce, cover, and refrigerate. *All advance preparation may be completed up to 8 hours before you begin the final cooking steps.*

FINAL COOKING STEPS

Place a wok over the highest heat. When the wok is very hot, add half of the cooking oil. Roll the oil around the wok to coat the inside, and when the oil gives off just a wisp of smoke, add the chicken. Stir and toss the chicken until it loses its raw exterior color, about 1 minute. Immediately transfer the chicken to a plate.

Immediately return the wok to highest heat. Add the remaining cooking oil and the garlic. Stir-fry the garlic and, as soon as it turns white, about 5 seconds, add the vegetables. Stir and toss the vegetables, adding the water to moisten the mushrooms. Stir-fry the vegetables until the asparagus turns bright green, about 2 minutes.

Stir the wok sauce, then pour it into the wok. Return the chicken to the wok. Add the pine nuts. Stir and toss until all the ingredients are glazed with the sauce. Taste and adjust the seasoning. Immediately transfer to a heated platter or 4 heated dinner plates and serve.

SUGGESTED ACCOMPANIMENTS

Broiled polenta, salad of field greens with walnut oil dressing, and hot peach cobbler

Caribbean Chicken Stir-Fry with Mint

For stir-frying, always marinate chicken for at least 15 minutes but not longer than 8 hours. The common marinade combination of Chinese rice wine and thin soy (to add flavor), a few teaspoons of cooking oil (to prevent the chicken from sticking to the sides of the wok), and, sometimes, a tiny amount of cornstarch (to stop the chicken from "steaming" in its own marinade when added to the wok) can be easily varied. Use no more than ¼ cup marinade for 1 pound of chicken. Try varying the marinade ingredients for this dish by choosing from the Caribbean seasonings of tamarind, mango concentrate, curry powder, finely minced chiles, garlic, ginger, and grated orange and lime zests.

Serves 4 as an entrée

INGREDIENTS

4 chicken breast halves, boned and skinned

2 tablespoons hoisin sauce

2 tablespoons Chinese rice wine or dry sherry

1 red bell pepper

3 whole green onions

½ cup lightly packed mint leaves

¼ cup mild olive oil

WOK SEASONINGS

3 cloves garlic, finely minced

1 tablespoon very finely minced ginger

WOK SAUCE

½ teaspoon finely minced orange zest

¼ cup freshly squeezed orange juice

3 tablespoons hoisin sauce

2 tablespoons dark rum

1 tablespoon packed light brown sugar

1 tablespoon cornstarch

2 teaspoons Caribbean chile sauce

¼ teaspoon ground allspice

¼ teaspoon ground nutmeg

ADVANCE PREPARATION

Cut the chicken breasts lengthwise into ½-inch-wide strips. Place the strips together and cut across them to make ¼-inch-wide pieces. Place the chicken in a small bowl, add the hoisin sauce and rice wine, and mix well. Cover and refrigerate at least 15 minutes but not longer than 8 hours.

Stem, derib, and seed the red pepper, then cut it into ½-inch squares. Cut the green onions on a sharp diagonal into ½-inch-long pieces. Combine the pepper and green onions and refrigerate. In separate containers, set aside the mint leaves and olive oil. In a small bowl, combine the wok seasoning ingredients. In another bowl, combine the wok sauce ingredients and stir well. *All advance preparation may be completed up to 8 hours before you begin the final cooking steps.*

FINAL COOKING STEPS

Place a wok over the highest heat. When the wok is very hot, add half the olive oil. Roll the oil around the wok to coat the insides, and when the oil gives off just a wisp of smoke, add the chicken. Stir and toss the chicken until it loses its raw exterior color, about 1 minute. Immediately transfer the chicken to a plate.

Immediately return the wok to the highest heat. Add the remaining olive oil and the wok seasonings. Stir-fry for about 5 seconds, then add the pepper and green onion. Stir and toss the vegetables until the red pepper brightens in color, about 2 minutes.

Stir the wok sauce, then pour it into the wok. Return the chicken to the wok. Add the mint leaves. Stir and toss until all the ingredients are glazed with the sauce. Taste and adjust the seasoning. Immediately transfer to a heated platter or 4 heated dinner plates and serve.

SUGGESTED ACCOMPANIMENTS

Saffron rice; spinach, avocado, and pecan salad; and ginger flan

Pan-Fried Chicken with Asian-Cajun Sauce

This is one of the simplest, most satisfying ways to cook chicken breast halves with the bone in and skin attached. Once the chicken breasts have been browned, the heat is lowered to medium, the pan is covered, and the chicken breasts are gently cooked for about 8 minutes. Sprinkled with a little salt and freshly ground black pepper, the chicken tastes excellent straight from the pan, or you may accompany the chicken breasts with a salsa, chutney, or, as in this recipe, with an Asian-Cajun mayonnaise flavored with Grand Marnier, lime, chile, fresh ginger, and chopped cilantro.

Serves 4 as an entrée

INGREDIENTS

6 to 8 chicken breast halves, bone in and skin on

1 teaspoon ground coriander

1 teaspoon dry mustard

1/4 teaspoon ground white pepper

1/2 teaspoon salt

1/2 cup unbleached all-purpose flour

1/3 cup cooking oil

2 limes, cut into wedges

1/2 cup mild Asian or Louisiana chile sauce

ASIAN-CAJUN SAUCE

1 cup mayonnaise

2 tablespoons Grand Marnier

1 tablespoon freshly squeezed lime juice

2 teaspoons Worcestershire sauce

1 teaspoon Asian chile sauce

1 tablespoon very finely minced ginger

1 teaspoon finely minced orange zest

2 tablespoons chopped cilantro sprigs

1/2 teaspoon salt

ADVANCE PREPARATION

Rinse chicken with cold water, then pat dry. Using a heavy knife or poultry shears, trim away any exposed rib bones, and cut away the wing sockets. Cut off and discard all excess fat. In a small bowl, combine the coriander, mustard, pepper, and salt. In separate bowls, set aside the flour, oil, lime wedges, and chile sauce. In another bowl combine all the ingredients for the Asian-Cajun Sauce, stir well, cover, and refrigerate. *All advance preparation may be completed up to 8 hours before you begin the final cooking steps.*

FINAL COOKING STEPS

Place a 14-inch sauté pan over medium-high heat. On a baking sheet or on a layer of waxed paper or parchment paper, place the chicken. Sprinkle the chicken pieces on both sides with the coriander mixture, then lightly dust the chicken pieces on both sides with flour, being sure to shake off all the excess flour.

Immediately add the oil to the sauté pan. When the oil is hot and shimmering but has not begun to smoke, add the chicken pieces, skin side up. Regulating the heat so that the oil constantly sizzles but never smokes, cook the chicken on both sides until golden, a total of about 8 minutes. Now reduce the heat to low, cover the pan, and cook the chicken about 10 to 15 minutes longer, turning each piece over once. The chicken is done when an instant-read meat thermometer registers 155 degrees when inserted deeply into the meat and the juices run clear when the chicken is pierced deeply with a fork.

Transfer the chicken to a heated platter or 4 heated dinner plates. Accompany with the lime wedges, chile sauce, and Asian-Cajun Sauce. Serve at once.

SUGGESTED ACCOMPANIMENTS

Baby roasted potatoes, watercress salad, and rhubarb cobbler

Chicken in Creole Tomato Cream Sauce

INGREDIENTS

8 chicken breast halves, boned but skin on
Salt and black pepper
½ cup unbleached all-purpose flour
1 tablespoon unsalted butter
2 tablespoons olive oil
3 cloves garlic, finely minced

CREOLE TOMATO CREAM SAUCE

2 vine ripened tomatoes
½ cup heavy cream
¼ cup dry vermouth
2 tablespoons oyster sauce
2 teaspoons Louisiana or Asian chile sauce
1 teaspoon sugar
2 tablespoons finely chopped fresh oregano
   leaves
1 tablespoon finely chopped fresh thyme

*T*his sauce has a beautiful balance of flavors. The sweet, slightly acidic flavor of vine-ripened tomatoes, the deep low-note flavor and slightly salty-tasting oyster sauce, the spicy high-note flavor of a small amount of chile sauce and chopped herbs, all work together so that no one flavor dominates and complex tastes reveal themselves after several bites. The heavy cream provides a "rounded mouthfeel" by causing all the flavors to linger on the palate. This sauce is great when added to pan-fried dumplings, combined with 4 cups of cooked pasta that is being sautéed, or when cooked on its own and then spooned over broiled or barbecued fish.

Serves 4 as an entrée

ADVANCE PREPARATION

Rinse the chicken with cold water, then pat dry. Trim off all excess skin from around the edges of the chicken, then place the chicken in a bowl, cover, and refrigerate. Set aside separately the salt, pepper, and flour. Combine the butter and oil and set aside. Set the garlic aside.

To make the cream sauce, submerge the tomatoes in boiling water for 5 seconds, then peel. Cut the tomatoes in half, gently squeeze out and discard the seeds, then chop the tomatoes finely. Transfer the tomatoes to a bowl and combine with the remaining ingredients. *All advance preparation may be completed up to 8 hours before you begin the final cooking steps.*

FINAL COOKING STEPS

Place a 12- or 14-inch sauté pan over medium-high heat. Sprinkle the chicken on both sides with a little salt and freshly ground black pepper, lightly coat both sides with flour, then shake each piece to remove any excess flour. When the pan is hot, add the butter and oil. When the butter begins to sizzle but has not browned, add the chicken, skin side down.

Regulating the heat so that the oil constantly sizzles but never smokes, cook the chicken until it is golden, about 4 minutes. Turn the chicken over and cook until it is firm to the touch and has just lost its raw interior color, about 4 minutes (an instant-read meat thermometer inserted deeply in the chicken should register 150 degrees and the juices should run clear when the chicken is pierced with a fork). Transfer the chicken (whole or sliced) to a heated platter or 4 heated dinner plates.

Discard all but 2 tablespoons of oil from the pan. Set the pan over medium-high heat and add the garlic. Sauté the garlic for 5 seconds, then add the tomato cream sauce. Bring the sauce to a high boil and cook until the sauce thickens slightly, about 1 minute. Taste and adjust the seasoning. Spoon the sauce over the chicken and serve at once.

SUGGESTED ACCOMPANIMENTS

Watercress salad and nectarine tart

Tangier Chicken with Tangerine Glaze

Rubbing a few seasonings across chicken before applying the protective coating of flour gives chicken a more complex taste. Here, a blend of cumin, cinnamon, paprika, and cayenne form a perfect flavor bridge between the chicken and the tangerine-herb sauce. The next time you sauté chicken, make your own flavor blend by choosing from your pantry of ground spices and crushed dried herbs. But don't rub the chicken with chopped fresh herbs, which blacken during sautéing.

Serves 4 as an entrée

INGREDIENTS

6 to 8 chicken breast halves, bone in and skin on

1 teaspoon ground cumin

½ teaspoon ground cinnamon

½ teaspoon sweet paprika

½ teaspoon cayenne pepper

½ teaspoon salt

½ cup unbleached all-purpose flour

3 tablespoons olive oil

3 tablespoons butter

½ cup raw hazelnuts

3 cloves garlic, finely minced

1 cup freshly squeezed tangerine juice

½ cup dry white wine

2 tablespoons honey

1 teaspoon Asian or Caribbean chile sauce

½ teaspoon salt

¼ cup slivered basil leaves

¼ cup chopped cilantro sprigs

4 teaspoons cornstarch

ADVANCE PREPARATION

Preheat the oven to 325 degrees (to toast the nuts). Rinse the chicken with cold water, then pat dry. Using a heavy knife or poultry shears, trim away any exposed rib bones, and cut away the wing sockets. Cut off and discard all excess fat. In a small bowl, combine the cumin, cinnamon, paprika, cayenne, and salt. In a separate bowl, set aside the flour. In another bowl, combine the olive oil and butter.

Place the nuts on a baking sheet, and toast in a preheated 325-degree oven for 15 minutes, or until golden. If the papery skins are still on the nuts, wrap them in a kitchen towel for a few minutes. Rub the towel vigorously between your palms until all skins have been removed. Chop the nuts very coarsely and set aside. In a small bowl set aside the minced garlic. In a small bowl, combine the tangerine juice and all the remaining ingredients. Stir well and set aside. *All advance preparation may be completed up to 8 hours before you begin the final cooking steps.*

FINAL COOKING STEPS

Place a 14-inch sauté pan over medium-high heat. On a baking sheet or layer of waxed paper or parchment paper, place the chicken. Sprinkle the chicken pieces on both sides with the cumin mixture, then lightly dust the chicken pieces on both sides with flour and shake off all excess flour.

Immediately add the oil and butter to the pan. When the butter melts and begins to sizzle, about 2 minutes, add the chicken pieces, skin side up. Cook the chicken on both sides until golden, a total cooking time of about 8 minutes. While browning the chicken, regulate the heat so that the oil constantly sizzles but never smokes. Now reduce the heat to low, cover the pan, and cook the chicken about 10 to 15 minutes longer, turning each piece once. The chicken is done when an instant-read meat thermometer registers 155 degrees when inserted deeply into the meat and the juices run clear when the chicken is pierced with a fork.

Transfer the chicken to a serving platter or 4 heated dinner plates. Spoon out all but 2 tablespoons of the oil, then place the pan over medium-high heat. Add the garlic and sauté for 10 seconds to cook lightly (but do not brown). Add the tangerine juice mixture and bring to a rapid boil. As soon as the mixture thickens, remove the pan from the heat, taste the sauce and adjust the seasoning, especially for salt, then spoon the sauce around the chicken pieces. Sprinkle with the nuts and serve at once.

SUGGESTED ACCOMPANIMENTS

Basmati rice pilaf, grilled squash, and banana ginger tart

*T*iming and good technique are the essence of this recipe, which must be marinated at least 8 hours in advance. The buttermilk tenderizes the chicken and helps the flavors of garlic, ginger, and chile permeate the meat. Carefully rolling the buttermilk-moistened chicken pieces individually in flour creates a batter. Drying the chicken pieces on a wire rack in the refrigerator for at least 45 minutes firms the batter and keeps it intact during cooking. Finally, pan-frying the chicken in a single layer in 2 or 3 batches and regulating the heat so that the oil temperature remains between 350 and 365 degrees yields truly magnificent taste and texture sensations. This dish is delicious either hot or cold.

Serves 4 as an entrée

Buttermilk-Crusted Chicken

I N G R E D I E N T S

2 small frying chickens, cut into pieces

2 cups buttermilk

2 cups finely chopped fresh parsley

6 cloves garlic, finely minced

¼ cup very finely minced ginger

1 tablespoon salt

2 teaspoons crushed red pepper (chile flakes)

3 cups unbleached all-purpose flour

Salt

2 cups cooking oil

1 star fruit (optional)

H A W A I I A N   S A L S A

1 nearly ripe papaya, peeled, seeded, and chopped

2 ripe kiwi, peeled and chopped

¼ fresh pineapple, peeled, cored, and chopped

¼ cup finely chopped cilantro sprigs

2 cloves garlic, finely minced

1 serrano chile, very finely minced (including the seeds)

2 tablespoons freshly squeezed orange juice

1 tablespoon packed light brown sugar

ADVANCE PREPARATION

Rinse the chicken pieces with cold water, then pat dry. In a bowl large enough to hold the chicken, combine the buttermilk, parsley, garlic, ginger, salt, and pepper flakes. Stir well. Add the chicken to the bowl and stir to coat evenly. Cover and refrigerate for at least 8 hours or overnight.

After marinating the chicken, place the white flour in a large bowl. Season the flour with a sprinkling of salt. Dip the chicken pieces, one at a time, into the flour, then shake off all the excess flour, and place the chicken on a wire rack. Refrigerate the chicken on the wire rack for at least 45 minutes or up to 8 hours. Set aside the oil and star fruit.

In a small bowl, combine all the ingredients for the Hawaiian salsa. Stir well and, if not using within 4 hours, cover and refrigerate. *All advance preparation may be completed up to 8 hours before you begin the final cooking steps.*

FINAL COOKING STEPS

Preheat the oven to 180 degrees to keep the cooked pieces of chicken warm. Place the oil in a 14-inch sauté pan over medium-high heat and heat the oil to 365 degrees or until bubbles surround the end of a wooden spoon when it is dipped into the oil. Place half the chicken, skin side down, in the hot oil. Regulating the heat so that the oil is constantly bubbling but never smoking, fry the chicken until golden on one side, about 10 minutes. Turn the pieces and cook until golden on the other side, about 10 more minutes. Turn the pieces once more and cook for about 5 minutes. The chicken is done when an instant-read meat thermometer inserted deeply into the meat registers 155 degrees for chicken breasts and 170 degrees for drumsticks and thighs and the juices run clear when the chicken is pierced with a fork. Drain the chicken on wire racks, then transfer to a heated platter or 4 heated dinner plates. Keep warm in the oven while cooking the rest of the chicken. Slice the star fruit. Serve at once, accompanied by the Hawaiian salsa and star fruit.

SUGGESTED ACCOMPANIMENTS

Garlic mashed potatoes, Caesar salad with chile croutons, and hot apple pie with bourbon ice cream

Vermouth Chicken with Shiitakes

This recipe uses a very practical technique common to restaurant chefs. Once the chicken breast has been browned in a sauté pan, the pan holding the chicken is transferred to a 375-degree oven to complete the cooking. Browning the chicken seals the juices inside, and cooking it in the oven liberates the cook from having to regulate the heat and turn the chicken over. Once the chicken finishes cooking, it is transferred to heated dinner plates and a sauce is quickly made in the hot pan. This method works whether using whole chicken breast halves or boned chicken breasts, with or without skin.

Serves 4 as an entrée

INGREDIENTS

6 to 8 chicken breast halves, boned but skin on

Black pepper

.30 ounce dried shiitake mushrooms

⅓ cup light olive oil

2 cloves garlic, finely minced

1 red bell pepper

4 ounces fresh shiitake mushrooms

1 cup heavy cream

½ cup dry vermouth

1 tablespoon oyster sauce

2 teaspoons dark sesame oil

½ teaspoon sugar

½ teaspoon Asian chile sauce

½ teaspoon grated orange zest

¼ cup chopped chives

ADVANCE PREPARATION

Rinse the chicken with cold water, then pat dry. Sprinkle the chicken lightly with freshly ground black pepper. Place the dried mushrooms in a spice grinder and pulverize until the mushrooms have the texture of sand. Coat the chicken breasts with the mushrooms, place the chicken on a wire rack, cover, and refrigerate.

Set aside the olive oil. Set aside the minced garlic. Remove and discard the stem, ribs, and seeds of the red pepper. Cut the pepper into 1-inch-long and ⅛-inch-wide matchstick-shaped pieces, then set aside. Remove and discard the shiitake mushroom stems, cut the caps into ¼-inch-wide strips, and set aside. In a bowl, combine all the remaining ingredients except the chives; set the chives aside in a separate bowl. *All of the advance preparation may be completed up to 8 hours before you begin the final cooking steps.*

FINAL COOKING STEPS

Preheat the oven to 375 degrees for the final cooking of the chicken. Place a 14-inch oven-proof sauté pan over medium-high heat. When the pan is hot, add half the olive oil. When the oil is hot, add the chicken in a single layer. Sauté the chicken until it is lightly browned, about 2 minutes on each side. Immediately cover the pan, and transfer it to the preheated oven. Cook the chicken until an instant-read meat thermometer registers 150 degrees when inserted deeply into a breast and the juices run clear when the chicken is pierced with a fork, about 5-8 minutes.

Transfer the chicken to a heated platter or 4 heated dinner plates. Immediately place the pan over high heat and add the remaining olive oil and the garlic. Sauté for 5 seconds, then add the red pepper and mushrooms. Sauté the mushrooms until they soften slightly, about 1 minute. Stir the sauce and bring the mixture to a rapid boil. Boil until the sauce begins to thicken enough to lightly coat a spoon, about 2 minutes. Taste and adjust the seasoning. Pour the sauce over the chicken, sprinkle with chives, and serve at once.

SUGGESTED ACCOMPANIMENTS

Caviar blintzes, wild rice, endive salad with candied walnuts, and strawberries romanoff norene

The chicken "tender," known as the "sprout" to the Chinese, is the long, thin fillet that lies between the bone and the large piece of breast meat. Increasingly available at supermarkets, these extremely tender morsels are great when flash-cooked in a sauté pan, cut crosswise into 1/4-inch pieces for stir-frying in a wok, or rubbed with one of the barbecue sauces from the previous chapter and seared on a grill or barbecue. Avoid roasting or broiling chicken tenders, however, because the meat quickly becomes very dry.

Serves 4 as an entrée

Thai Town Chicken

INGREDIENTS

1½ pounds chicken tenders

Salt and black pepper

½ cup unbleached all-purpose flour

¼ cup cooking oil

3 cloves garlic, finely minced

1 tablespoon very finely minced ginger

2 serrano chiles, finely minced (including the seeds)

4 ounces button mushrooms

½ teaspoon finely minced orange zest

½ cup freshly squeezed orange juice

¼ cup Chinese rice wine or dry sherry

2 tablespoons Thai fish sauce

1 tablespoon cornstarch

2 tablespoons mint leaves

2 tablespoons chopped fresh chives

ADVANCE PREPARATION

Wash the tenders with cold water, then pat dry. Cut off and discard the white tendons, then refrigerate the tenders. Set aside the salt, pepper, and flour. Set aside separately the cooking oil. In a small bowl, combine the garlic, ginger, and chiles; set aside. Thinly slice the mushrooms into ⅛-inch-wide pieces, and set aside. In small bowl, combine the minced orange zest, orange juice, rice wine, fish sauce, and cornstarch. *All advance preparation may be completed up to 8 hours before you begin the final cooking steps.*

FINAL COOKING STEPS

Finely chop the mint and chives, and set aside. Place a 12-inch sauté pan over medium-high heat. Sprinkle the chicken pieces on all sides with a little salt and freshly ground black pepper. Sprinkle on the flour, lightly dusting the pieces, then shake each piece to remove all excess flour.

When the pan is hot, add half of the cooking oil. When the oil is hot and shimmering, add the chicken tenders in a single layer. Sauté the chicken for about 2 minutes on each side.

Regulating the heat so the oil is constantly sizzling but not smoking, cook chicken until it is firm to the touch and has just lost its raw interior color. Immediately transfer the chicken to a heated platter or 4 heated dinner plates.

Immediately place the pan over high heat, and add the remaining cooking oil, garlic, ginger, and chiles. Sauté the seasonings for 15 seconds, then add the mushrooms. Stir and toss the mushrooms until they soften slightly. Stir the orange juice mixture and add to the pan. Bring the liquid to a rapid boil and cook until it thickens slightly, about 1 minute. Stir in the mint and chives. Taste and adjust the seasoning. Spoon the sauce over the chicken and serve at once.

SUGGESTED ACCOMPANIMENTS

Fresh tomato and basil salad, coconut rice, and pineapple Grand Marnier cake

Hot Chicken Crisp and Golden from the Oven

No other techniques are easier and more widely used for chicken than roasting and broiling. We'll show you how to roll chicken breasts stuffed with smoked Jarlsberg cheese and hours later to use a combination of broiling and roasting so that the skin becomes crisp while the delicate chicken breast meat cooks evenly. There are two stuffing recipes: one for a Middle Eastern stuffing made with rice, saffron, and currants, and the other for a wild mushroom stuffing placed between the chicken skin and meat. We'll explain why there is no better way to roast a whole unstuffed chicken than by placing the chicken on a vertical roaster, and give you a fail-proof method for roasting chicken pieces. Recipe after recipe will show you wonderful ways to make quick sauces that elevate ordinary roasted and broiled chicken to a sublime taste sensation.

For roasting, use a shallow, heavy roasting pan that distributes the heat evenly. Place the chicken on a nonstick wire rack that rests on the top edges of the roasting pan. This allows the hot oven air to circulate around the chicken and crisp the skin. Roast chicken in a preheated 425-degree oven. A hotter oven causes the drippings to burn, and in a cooler oven the skin will not crisp. Roast chicken pieces, skin side up, and do not turn them during roasting. Since chicken breasts cook more quickly than the legs, when roasting chicken pieces, place the breasts in the oven 10 minutes after you start to roast the legs. When roasting only chicken breasts (bone in and skin on), roast in a 375-degree oven because the lower heat keeps the meat more moist. Be sure to purchase the same size chicken breasts that are well-covered with skin. Once the chicken breasts reach an internal temperature of 150 degrees, turn the oven setting to broil and brown the skin (about 2 to 3 minutes). Don't roast boneless chicken breasts, because they become too dry.

If the chicken has not been marinated, sprinkle it with salt and freshly ground black pepper on all sides and in the cavity. During roasting, baste the chicken twice with the marinade or, if the chicken has not been marinated, brush the chicken with oil or melted butter.

To broil, preheat the oven to 400 degrees. Broil only boneless skin-on chicken breasts. Bone-in chicken pieces take considerably longer to cook, which greatly increases the chances that the meat and/or skin will burn. Once the oven has been preheated, turn the setting to broil and cook the chicken 4 inches from the heating element of the broiler. Cook the chicken, skin side up, until the skin becomes golden and crisp, then turn the chicken over, and continue broiling until the internal temperature reaches 150 degrees when an instant-read meat thermometer is inserted deeply into the chicken. If using an electric oven, keep the oven door ajar while broiling. (Otherwise the oven may become so hot that the broiler will shut off.)

With a little advance planning you will find it simple to assemble and cook this elegant dish—your friends will think you're a cooking hero! Ask your butcher to provide you with thinly pounded chicken breast halves that have plenty of extra skin around the sides. Next purchase a top-quality smoked cheese such as smoked Gouda (cut from a wheel, not highly processed Gouda cut from a loaf, which will not melt during roasting), imported smoked Jarlsberg, or a braided imported Italian smoked mozzarella (**scamorzza**). Stuff, roll, and tie the breasts in the morning, then complete the simple roasting instructions that evening.

Serves 4 as an entrée

Chicken Breasts Stuffed with Smoked Gouda

INGREDIENTS

8 green Anaheim chiles

8 chicken breast halves, boned but skin on, pounded thinly

Salt and freshly ground black pepper to taste

1 teaspoon ground cumin

¼ cup finely chopped cilantro sprigs

6 ounces smoked Gouda, shredded

¼ cup salted toasted pumpkin seeds

¼ cup olive oil

SALSA

5 vine-ripened tomatoes (about 1½ pounds), seeded and chopped

½ cup chopped green onions

½ cup chopped cilantro sprigs

2 cloves garlic cloves, finely minced

1 tablespoon very finely minced ginger

3 tablespoons white wine vinegar

2 tablespoons dark sesame oil

1 tablespoon safflower oil

1½ teaspoons sugar

1 teaspoon Asian chile sauce

½ teaspoon salt

ADVANCE PREPARATION

Place the whole chiles over a gas burner turned to high and roast until blackened on all sides, or place them under a preheated broiler, and broil until blackened. As soon as the chiles are roasted, place them in a plastic or paper bag, and close the bag. After 5 minutes, remove the chiles and rub off the black skin. Discard the stem, and cut the chiles lengthwise so that each one opens into a flat piece. Discard the chiles' seeds and ribs.

Rinse the chicken breasts with cold water, then pat dry. Lay the chicken breasts, skin side down, on a work surface and sprinkle the meat with the salt, pepper, cumin, and chopped cilantro. Place a single chile on each breast, then add a thin layer of shredded Gouda. Tightly roll each breast. Loop 1 or 2 pieces of string around each breast and tie it snugly so that the cylinder is held closed. Cover and refrigerate.

In separate containers, set aside the pumpkin seeds and olive oil. Combine all the ingredients for the salsa, stir well, and set aside at room temperature. *All advance preparation may be completed up to 8 hours before you begin the final cooking steps.*

FINAL COOKING STEPS

Preheat the oven to 450 degrees. Line a shallow roasting pan with aluminum foil, then top the pan with a wire rack that has been sprayed with vegetable-oil cooking spray. Place the chicken, skin side up, on the wire rack. Turn the oven setting to broil, place the chicken approximately 4 inches below the heating element of the broiler, and broil the chicken until the skin is golden, about 4 to 6 minutes. Immediately turn the oven to 400 degrees. Brush the chicken with olive oil and roast it for approximately 15 minutes longer. The chicken is done when an instant-read meat thermometer registers 155 degrees when inserted deeply into the breast and the juices run clear when the chicken is pierced with a fork.

Warm the salsa if you wish. Spoon the salsa across 4 heated dinner plates. Place the chicken in the center of the salsa, sprinkle with the toasted pumpkin seeds, and serve at once.

SUGGESTED ACCOMPANIMENTS

Wild rice with currants, Asian papaya salad, and peach sundaes

Lemon Chicken with a Chile Accent

Classic Chinese lemon chicken is one of the world's great culinary triumphs. Strips of chicken are dipped in a tempuralike batter, deep-fried until golden and crisp, then cut into bite-sized pieces and drizzled with lemon sauce—all of which requires perfect timing and several last-minute cooking steps. In this recipe the chicken pieces are brushed with a spicy lemon butter during roasting, and the roast chicken is glazed with a complexly flavored lemon sauce. Lemon juice deteriorates quickly, so be sure to squeeze the lemons within hours of use and keep the juice refrigerated.

Serves 4 as an entrée

INGREDIENTS

2 frying chickens, cut into pieces

1 cup lightly packed cilantro sprigs

½ cup (1 stick) unsalted butter, at room temperature

4 cloves garlic

¼ cup thinly sliced ginger

1 tablespoon finely minced lemon zest (about 1 lemon)

2 teaspoons salt

2 teaspoons crushed red chile (chile flakes)

LEMON SAUCE

2 teaspoons finely minced lemon zest

½ cup freshly squeezed lemon juice

½ cup chicken stock

6 tablespoons sugar

2 tablespoons thin soy sauce

2 tablespoons cornstarch

½ teaspoon salt

ADVANCE PREPARATION

Rinse the chicken with cold water, then pat dry and refrigerate. Finely chop enough cilantro to fill ¼ cup. Set aside the remaining cilantro to use as a garnish. Cut the butter into 8 pieces. In a food processor, finely mince the garlic and ginger. Add the chopped cilantro, butter, minced lemon zest, salt, and pepper flakes. Process until evenly blended. Pack the lemon butter into a small dish, cover, and refrigerate.

In a small saucepan, combine all the ingredients for the Lemon Sauce, cover, and refrigerate. *All advance preparation may be completed up to 8 hours before you begin the final cooking steps.*

FINAL COOKING STEPS

Preheat the oven to 425 degrees. Line a shallow roasting pan with aluminum foil and top the roasting pan with a wire rack that has been sprayed with vegetable-oil cooking spray. Place the chicken, skin side up, on the wire rack. Melt the lemon butter, then brush the butter over the chicken. Roast the chicken for approximately 30 minutes, brushing on more lemon butter after 15 minutes of roasting. The chicken is done when an instant-read meat thermometer registers 155 degrees for breasts and 170 degrees for thighs and the juices run clear when the chicken is pierced with a fork.

Transfer the chicken to a heated platter or 4 heated dinner plates. Place the Lemon Sauce over high heat and bring to a low boil, stirring. As soon as the sauce thickens, about 1 minute, spoon it over the chicken pieces. Garnish with cilantro and serve at once.

SUGGESTED ACCOMPANIMENTS

Saffron bowtie pasta, red pepper and feta salad, and chocolate orange mousse

- Sautéed boneless chicken breasts should be browned in about $1/16$ inch of oil and/or butter. If less oil or butter is used, the outside of the chicken will be dry and stringy, and will not brown uniformly.

- When preparing chicken for sautéing use flour, cornstarch, an equal mixture of cornstarch and flour, bread crumbs, unsalted cracker crumbs, or unsweetened cereal crumbs to coat the chicken. Coating chicken can be messy. Place the flour or the other coatings in a paper bag, add the chicken, and shake the bag vigorously. As you remove the chicken from the bag, knock the pieces together to dislodge all excess coating.

- One of the best ways to cook either bone-in or boneless chicken breasts, with the skin, is to dust the chicken with flour, brown it on both sides in $1/16$ inch of oil, then spoon out the oil, cover the pan, and transfer the pan to a preheated 375-degree oven. Cook bone-in breasts for 15 minutes and boneless skin-on breasts for 10 minutes. The chicken will be marvelously tender, with an intense chicken flavor.

- To reduce the amount of time it takes to fry chicken, transfer the chicken to a wire rack as soon as the batter turns golden and finish cooking it in a preheated 350-degree oven. The batter will still be detectably crisp.

- For great chicken stock, freeze all the chicken trimmings, giblets, and bones. Once you have accumulated a few pounds, defrost the scraps, place them in a stockpot, cover them with water, and bring to a simmer. Skim off the froth that rises to the surface, then simmer the chicken for 1 to 5 hours. Now strain, cool, and remove the fat with pieces of paper towels. Refrigerate the stock, bringing it to a boil for 5 minutes every fourth day, or freeze.

- If chicken has not been marinated, always salt and pepper the skin and the inside of the body cavity of a whole chicken. But do not put salt directly on the chicken meat because it will extract moisture and cause the meat to become dry.

- Because white meat cooks more quickly than dark meat, when roasting or barbecuing chicken pieces, add chicken breasts 5 minutes after beginning to cook chicken legs and thighs.

- Butterfly chicken for barbecuing and roasting. Ask your butcher to butterfly the chicken down the backbone and to flatten the chicken into an even thickness by pushing down on the breastbone and pounding the chicken with a flat mallet. If you place a heavy weight, such as a piece of cinder block wrapped with foil, on the chicken during barbecuing or roasting, the chicken will cook more quickly and brown more evenly.

- Once bone-in chicken pieces have been barbecued, grilled, roasted, or sautéed, let the chicken rest for 5 minutes. This allows the meat to absorb juices that otherwise would escape, and the meat will thus be more tender and more moist. Boneless chicken pieces, which cool quickly, should be served at once.

Hot Chicken Cooking Tips

One of the best devices for roasting chicken is the nonstick vertical roaster. Shaped like an inverted funnel that fits snugly inside the cavity, the chicken stands upright and the metal funnel distributes heat and sears the cavity. While the hot oven air circulates around the upright chicken, fat from the breast skin bastes the bird, keeping the breast meat moist, and the skin becomes crisp all over.

Serves 4 as an entrée

Spicy Citrus Chicken with Winter Vegetables

INGREDIENTS

1 4½-pound roasting chicken

12 mixed golden or red baby beets

1 bunch baby turnips

12 small red and yellow potatoes

1 bunch of baby carrots

1 fennel bulb

½ cup cilantro sprigs for garnish

SPICY CITRUS MARINADE

2 tablespoons finely minced orange zest

1 cup freshly squeezed orange juice

⅔ cup hoisin sauce

¼ cup honey

6 cloves garlic, finely minced

¼ cup very finely minced ginger

½ cup minced whole green onions

ADVANCE PREPARATION

Rinse the chicken with cold water and pat dry. Remove and discard the fat pads lying on each side of the body cavity. Gently push your index finger underneath the skin lying along the front edge of the cavity, being careful to make as small an opening as possible. Then carefully slide your finger underneath the skin to loosen the skin covering the breast, thigh, and drumstick.

In a small bowl, combine all the ingredients for the marinade. Stir well. Holding the chicken upright so it rests on the neck end, spoon or pour about ½ cup of the marinade under the skin. Using your fingers, gently massage the skin in order to help the marinade spread under the breast, thigh, and drumstick skin. Place the chicken on a plate and gently rub about half the remaining marinade across the outside of the chicken as well as in the cavity. Cover and refrigerate the chicken for at least 30 minutes or up to 8 hours. Reserve the rest of the marinade to use later as a basting sauce.

Trim the top and bottom of the beets and turnips. Scrub vigorously and set aside. Scrub the potatoes and set aside. Trim and scrub the carrots. Trim off the ends of the fennel bulb, then cut the bulb into quarters. Set the cilantro sprigs aside. *All advance preparation may be completed up to 8 hours before you begin the final cooking steps.*

FINAL COOKING STEPS

Remove the chicken from the refrigerator 30 minutes before roasting. Preheat the oven to 375 degrees. Line a shallow roasting pan with aluminum foil and spray the foil with a vegetable-oil cooking spray. Stand the vertical roaster upright in the pan and gently position the chicken on the vertical roaster. Scatter the beets, potatoes, carrots, and fennel around the chicken. Place the roasting pan in the preheated oven and roast the chicken for approximately 60 minutes, basting the chicken and the root vegetables every 15 minutes with the reserved marinade. The chicken is done when an instant-read meat thermometer registers 170 degrees when inserted deeply into a thigh and the juices run clear when the chicken is pierced with a fork.

Remove the chicken from the oven and transfer it to a carving board. Let the chicken rest for 5 minutes, then cut the chicken into pieces using a knife or poultry shears. Transfer the chicken pieces to 4 heated dinner plates, add the root vegetables, garnish with cilantro, and serve at once.

SUGGESTED ACCOMPANIMENTS

Spinach salad with walnut dressing and raspberry crème brûlée

Chicken with Cognac and Wild Mushroom Stuffing

*C*hicken skin, condemned by some as "unhealthy," nevertheless plays a starring role in many chicken recipes. Whether for sautéing, barbecuing, roasting, or broiling, crisply cooked skin shields the meat from intense heat while keeping it moist by providing a natural basting essence. Several of this book's recipes sandwich a marinade between the skin and meat, but here a stuffing is carefully positioned under the skin to infuse the meat with its own special flavor. For the bread crumbs, use a good baguette of French or sourdough bread, sliced and chopped into small pieces.

Serves 4 as an entrée

INGREDIENTS

2 frying chickens, split in half

4 cloves garlic, finely minced

2 shallots, finely minced

8 ounces mushrooms (shiitakes, chanterelles, morels, or buttons)

2 whole green onions

1/3 cup currants

2 cups 1/4-inch bread cubes

1/2 cup Cognac

1/2 cup chicken stock

1 tablespoon oyster sauce

1/2 teaspoon sugar

1/4 teaspoon freshly ground black pepper

2 tablespoons finely chopped fresh thyme

1/4 cup pine nuts

4 tablespoons unsalted butter

Salt and freshly ground pepper to taste

ADVANCE PREPARATION

Preheat the oven to 325 degrees (to toast the nuts). Rinse the chicken with cold water, then pat dry. Set the garlic and shallots aside. If using shiitake mushrooms, cut off and discard the stems. Cut the shiitakes or the other mushrooms into 1/8-inch-wide slices and set aside. Chop the green onions and set aside. Combine and set aside the currants and bread cubes. Set aside half of the Cognac. In a small bowl, combine the remaining Cognac, the stock, oyster sauce, sugar, pepper, and thyme. Toast the pine nuts in the preheated oven until the nuts turn light golden, about 8 minutes.

Place a 12-inch skillet or sauté pan over medium heat. When the pan is hot, add the butter. When the butter has melted and begins to sizzle, add the garlic and shallots. Sauté for 30 seconds, then add the mushrooms. Stir and toss the mushrooms until they begin to soften, about 5 minutes. Add the green onions, currants, and bread cubes and stir to mix evenly. Stir in the Cognac mixture and pine nuts. Stir until the bread crumbs are well moistened and all the liquid disappears, about 2 minutes. Taste the stuffing and adjust the seasoning, especially for salt and pepper. Place the stuffing on a plate and let cool to room temperature.

Separate the chicken skin from the meat of each chicken by gently pushing your index finger underneath the breast skin, then moving it along the breast, thigh, and drumstick, being careful not to dislodge the skin attached to the backbone. Rub the Cognac under the chicken skin. When the stuffing is at room temperature, gently push one fourth of the stuffing under the skin of each chicken half, so that the stuffing is spread evenly under the breast, thigh, and drumstick. *You may cover and refrigerate the chicken for up to 4 hours before you begin the final cooking steps.*

FINAL COOKING STEPS

Preheat the oven to 425 degrees. Line a shallow roasting pan with aluminum foil, and top the roasting pan with a wire rack that has been sprayed with vegetable-oil cooking spray. Lay the chicken, bone side down, on the rack, sprinkle skin with salt and pepper and roast approximately 30 minutes. The chicken is done when an instant-read meat thermometer registers 170 degrees when inserted deeply into a thigh and the juices run clear when the chicken is pierced with a fork. Remove the chicken from the oven. Cut the four chicken pieces in half, or separate the legs from the breast and wing portion. Transfer the chicken to a heated serving platter or 4 heated dinner plates and serve at once.

SUGGESTED ACCOMPANIMENTS

Baby roast potatoes, watercress and goat cheese salad, and ginger layer cake

The technique for roasting chicken wings is the same as the one used for roasting chicken pieces and chicken halves. Cooking the wings on a wire rack placed on a baking sheet allows the hot oven air to circulate around the wings and keeps them crisp. Although many supermarkets sell "drumettes" made from chicken wings, these are never as tender as whole chicken wings with the tips trimmed off.

Serves 4 to 10 as an appetizer, 2 as an entrée

Cajun Buffalo Wings

INGREDIENTS

- 3 pounds chicken wings
- 1 cup mild tomato-chile sauce
- 6 tablespoons honey
- ¼ cup red wine vinegar
- 2 tablespoons Worcestershire sauce
- 1 tablespoon crushed red pepper (chile flakes)
- 6 cloves garlic, finely minced
- ¼ cup finely chopped fresh cilantro
- ¼ cup minced whole green onion

ADVANCE PREPARATION

Rinse the chicken wings with cold water, then pat them dry. Cut the tips off the chicken wings and discard or save them for making stock. In a medium-sized bowl, combine all the remaining ingredients. Mix well and add the chicken wings, mix to coat them evenly, cover, and refrigerate. *All advance preparation may be completed up to 24 hours before you begin the final cooking steps.*

FINAL COOKING STEPS

Preheat the oven to 375 degrees. Line a baking sheet with aluminum foil, and top with a wire rack that has been sprayed with vegetable-oil cooking spray. Each chicken wing has a side whose skin is smoother and more attractive than the other side. Lay the wings on the rack with the attractive side down, and roast in the oven for 30 minutes. Baste the wings, turn them over, and baste the other side. Roast the wings for another 30 minutes, or until they are a deep mahogany color.

Remove the wings from the oven. With a knife or poultry shears, cut the wings in half through the joint. Serve at once.

SUGGESTED ACCOMPANIMENTS

Corn bread with garlic-herb butter, baby greens with Caesar dressing, and lemon meringue pie with caramel crust

Tropical Chicken with Grand Marnier

INGREDIENTS

6 to 8 chicken breast halves, bone in and skin on

2 tablespoons unsalted butter

1 tablespoon cooking oil

2 tablespoons very finely minced ginger

1 red bell pepper, stemmed, deribbed, seeded, and cubed

3 small whole green onions cut into 1-inch lengths

¼ pineapple, peeled, cored, and cubed

1 large ripe mango, peeled and cubed

½ cup dark raisins

½ cup chicken stock

⅓ cup Grand Marnier

2 teaspoons Caribbean or Asian chile sauce

2 teaspoons cornstarch

½ teaspoon ground allspice

½ teaspoon freshly grated nutmeg

½ teaspoon salt

¼ cup cilantro sprigs

¼ cup mint leaves

4 firm baby bananas

1 lime

In this recipe the mild taste of chicken serves as the stage on which the Caribbean flavors of allspice, nutmeg, tropical fruits, cilantro, and mint perform their starring roles. Except for bananas, choose fruit at the peak of freshness. To select a ripe pineapple, look for one that is slightly soft when you squeeze it gently. Pick soft mangoes that have a faint smell and a deep red blush across one third of the fruit. If mangoes are unavailable, choose ripe nectarines or peaches, but do not substitute papaya because it has an unexciting flavor when heated. As for the bananas, perfectly ripe bananas, whether regular or small sized, are mushy when heated. Buy firm bananas.

Serves 4 as an entrée

ADVANCE PREPARATION

Rinse the chicken with cold water, then pat dry. Using poultry shears or a heavy knife, trim away all exposed rib bones and cut away the wing sockets; then cover and refrigerate the breasts. In a small container, combine and set aside the butter, oil, and gingerroot. Combine and refrigerate the pepper, green onions, and pineapple. Combine and refrigerate the mango and raisins.

In a small bowl, combine the chicken stock, Grand Marnier, chile sauce, cornstarch, allspice, nutmeg, and salt; cover and refrigerate. Combine and set aside the cilantro and mint. Set aside the bananas. *All advance preparation may be completed up to 8 hours before you begin the final cooking steps.*

FINAL COOKING STEPS

Preheat the oven to 375 degrees. Line a shallow roasting pan with aluminum foil, then top the pan with a wire rack that has been sprayed with vegetable-oil cooking spray. Place the chicken breasts, skin side up, on the wire rack. Sprinkle with salt and pepper. Roast the chicken for approximately 20 to 25 minutes. The chicken is done when an instant-read meat thermometer registers 155 degrees when inserted deeply into the breast and the juices run clear when the chicken is pierced with a fork. Sprinkle the top of the chicken lightly with salt, then transfer it to a heated serving platter or 4 heated dinner plates.

Within 10 minutes of serving the dish, finely chop the cilantro and mint. Peel the bananas and split them in half lengthwise. Cut the lime into wedges. Place a 12-inch skillet or sauté pan over high heat. When the pan is hot, add the butter, oil, and ginger. When the ginger begins to sizzle, add the pepper, green onions, and pineapple. Stir and toss until the peppers brighten in color and the pineapple is lightly browned. Add the mangoes, raisins, and bananas and cook for 30 seconds. Add the Grand Marnier mixture. Immediately stir in the cilantro and mint. Taste and adjust the seasoning. Spoon the fruit around the chicken and serve at once with lime wedges.

SUGGESTED ACCOMPANIMENTS

Coconut basmati rice, watercress salad, and black-and-white bread pudding

Slices of roast chicken served with stuffing and embellished with a simple pan sauce make an impressive entrée. Because the finishing touches for this recipe require about 10 minutes in the kitchen, choose side dishes that require no last-minute attention, and serve this dish for your family or a few close friends who can keep you company in the kitchen, lending moral support and perhaps a helping hand. Once the chicken has been removed from the oven, let it rest at room temperature for 5 to 10 minutes so that the meat absorbs the juices. Otherwise the juices will escape onto the cutting board and the chicken will not be as tender.

Serves 4 as an entrée

Middle Eastern Stuffed Chicken

INGREDIENTS

One 5-pound roasting chicken

½ cup unsalted butter

4 cups chicken stock

2 tree-ripened peaches

Salt and freshly ground pepper to taste

1 cup long-grain white rice (not Minute Rice)

½ teaspoon ground cinnamon

1 teaspoon salt

½ teaspoon freshly ground black pepper

½ cup slivered almonds

3 cloves garlic, finely minced

½ cup currants

⅓ cup finely chopped fresh parsley

⅓ cup chopped whole green onion

¼ cup finely chopped cilantro sprigs

1 tablespoon freshly squeezed lemon juice

ADVANCE PREPARATION

Preheat the oven to 325 degrees (to toast the nuts). Rinse the chicken with cold water, pat dry, then cover and refrigerate. Divide the butter in half and place in 2 containers. Divide the stock in half, place in 2 containers, cover, and refrigerate. Set aside the peaches, salt, and pepper.

Place the rice in a fine-meshed sieve and rinse with cold water until the water is no longer cloudy, then drain thoroughly. In a bowl combine 2 cups of the chicken stock, cinnamon, salt, and pepper. Place the almonds on a baking sheet and toast in the reheated oven until golden, about 15 minutes. Place an 8-cup saucepan over medium-high heat. Add half the butter. When the butter melts, add the garlic. Sauté the garlic for 15 seconds, then add the rice and currants. Stir for 3 minutes, then add the chicken stock mixture and bring to a low boil. Stir the rice, cover, reduce the heat to low, and simmer the rice for 18 minutes. Turn the rice into a bowl and let cool to room temperature. Stir in the parsley, green onion, cilantro, and almonds. *All advance preparation may be completed up to 8 hours before you begin the final cooking steps.*

FINAL COOKING STEPS

Peel, pit, and slice the peaches. Toss the peaches with the lemon juice and refrigerate. Preheat the oven to 350 degrees. In a small saucepan, melt the remaining butter. Stuff the chicken with the rice mixture. Truss the chicken to close. Spray a shallow roasting pan with vegetable-oil cooking spray. Place the chicken in the center of the roasting pan and roast it for about 1 hour and 20 minutes, brushing the chicken with melted butter every 15 minutes. The chicken is done when an instant-read meat thermometer registers 170 degrees when inserted deeply into a thigh and the juices run clear when the chicken is pierced with a fork.

Transfer the chicken to a carving board. Pour all but 3 tablespoons of the fat from the roasting pan. Place the roasting pan over medium-high heat, add the peaches, and sauté for 30 seconds. Add the remaining chicken stock and bring it to a vigorous boil. Scrape the pan to incorporate all the pan drippings into the chicken stock, and cook to reduce the liquid to about 1 cup. Season the pan sauce with salt and pepper and set aside.

Scoop the stuffing from the inside of the chicken and transfer the stuffing to 4 heated dinner plates. Alternatively, place the stuffing in individual ramekins, invert on the dinner plates, and remove the ramekins. Carve the chicken or cut it into pieces using poultry shears. Transfer the chicken to the dinner plates, spoon the peach sauce over, and serve at once.

SUGGESTED ACCOMPANIMENTS

Cucumber fennel root salad and mint swirl ice cream

Pecan Chicken with Grilled Tomatoes

If you want to roast chicken pieces without the skin, a protective coating must be added in order to shield the meat from the dry oven heat. This is done by dusting the chicken with flour, dipping each piece individually in egg, then rolling the pieces in finely ground nuts (pecans, hazelnuts, cashews) or bread crumbs. Don't use ground almonds, which are too dry, or ground walnuts, which often taste bitter. The coating has a more intense nut flavor when the nuts are toasted in the oven after being finely minced.

Serves 4 as an entrée

INGREDIENTS

6 chicken drumsticks, skinned

6 chicken thighs, skinned

1 tablespoon ground coriander

1 teaspoon crushed red pepper (chile flakes)

3 teaspoons salt

3 cups pecans

2 cups unbleached all-purpose flour

4 eggs, well beaten

GRILLED TOMATO SAUCE

3 tablespoons extra virgin olive oil

3 cloves garlic, finely minced

1½ vine-ripened tomatoes

½ green Anaheim chile

1 ear white corn

1 cup chicken stock

¼ cup finely chopped cilantro sprigs

½ teaspoon Asian chile sauce

½ teaspoon sugar

½ teaspoon salt

½ teaspoon finely minced lime zest

¼ teaspoon ground cinnamon

ADVANCE PREPARATION

Preheat the oven to 325 degrees (to toast the nuts). Line a baking sheet with aluminum foil. Rinse the chicken with cold water, then pat dry. Combine the coriander, pepper flakes, and 1 teaspoon of the salt; rub the chicken with the mixture. Spread the nuts on a baking sheet and toast them in the preheated oven until the nuts darken, about 15 minutes. Transfer the nuts to a bowl, stir in the remaining 2 teaspoons salt, and let cool to room temperature. Place the pecans in a food processor, and mince until finely ground. Place the ground pecans, flour, and beaten eggs in separate containers. Coat the outside of a chicken piece with flour, shaking off the excess. Dip it in the egg, roll in the pecans, and transfer to a wire rack placed on the foil-lined baking sheet. Repeat this process with remaining chicken pieces. Refrigerate the chicken on the wire rack for at least 1 hour but not more than 8 hours.

To make the tomato sauce, combine and set aside the oil and garlic. Place a grill pan over medium-high heat and, when hot, spray with a vegetable-oil cooking spray. Cut the tomatoes into ¼-inch-wide slices. Grill the tomatoes, chile, and corn until they become lightly charred. Chop the tomato. Stem, seed, derib, and cut the chile into ¼-inch cubes. Cut the kernels off the corn. In a bowl, combine the tomatoes, chile, corn, and remaining sauce ingredients, then set aside. *All advance preparation may be completed up to 8 hours before you begin the final cooking steps.*

FINAL COOKING STEPS

Preheat the oven to 425 degrees. Transfer the chicken, still on the wire rack, to the oven and bake until an instant-read meat thermometer registers 170 degrees when inserted deeply into a thigh and the juices run clear when the chicken is pierced with a fork, about 30 minutes. Remove from the pan.

Place a 12-inch skillet or sauté pan over medium-high heat. Add the oil and garlic. Sauté the garlic until it just begins to sizzle, then add the tomato sauce. Sauté for 30 seconds, taste and adjust the seasoning, then transfer the sauce to 4 heated dinner plates. Place the chicken on top of the sauce and serve at once.

SUGGESTED ACCOMPANIMENTS

Grilled baby corn, avocado jicama salad, and death by chocolate

hen planning to make a sauce from pan drippings that become fastened to the surface of a pan during roasting, choose a heavy roasting pan. Thin roasting pans cause the drippings to burn on the bottom of the pan and will tend to buckle when transferred from the oven to the stove top. As you bring the sauce to a boil in the pan, scrape the bottom vigorously with a metal or wooden spoon until the surface of the pan feels smooth and the sauce becomes richer in color. In this recipe, a portion of the marinade is stirred into the coconut sauce, adding an intense flavor.

Serves 4 as an entrée

Chicken Trinidad

INGREDIENTS

2 2½-pound fryers, split in half

1 cup cilantro sprigs

1 cup mint leaves

7 cloves garlic, finely minced

3 tablespoons very finely minced ginger

6 tablespoons thin soy sauce

6 tablespoons Grand Marnier

6 tablespoons honey

Finely minced zest from 1 lime

6 tablespoons freshly squeezed lime juice

3 tablespoons olive oil

1 tablespoon Caribbean chile sauce

1½ teaspoons ground allspice

½ cup coconut milk

½ cup chicken stock

2 tablespoons unsalted butter

8 firm baby bananas

ADVANCE PREPARATION

Rinse the chicken with cold water, then pat dry. Chop enough of the cilantro and mint to yield ¼ cup each. Set aside remaining cilantro sprigs and mint leaves. In a larger bowl, make a marinade by combining the minced cilantro and mint, the garlic, ginger, soy sauce, Grand Marnier, honey, lime zest, lime juice, oil, chile sauce, and allspice. Stir well, then combine ½ cup of the marinade with the coconut milk and chicken stock, cover, and refrigerate.

Working with one chicken half, loosen a small area of the skin along the top of the breast. Gently push your index finger underneath the skin, moving it along the breast, thigh, and drumstick, being careful not to dislodge the skin attached to the backbone. Repeat with the remaining chicken halves. Spoon 3 tablespoons of the marinade under the skin of one chicken half and, with your fingers, massage the outside of the skin to work the marinade over the breast, thigh, and drumstick. Rub another 3 tablespoons of the marinade over the entire outside surface of the chicken half. Repeat with the rest of the chicken halves. Cover and refrigerate at least 30 minutes but not more than 8 hours.

Set aside the butter and the bananas. *All advance preparation may be completed up to 8 hours before you begin the final cooking steps.*

FINAL COOKING STEPS

Preheat the oven to 425 degrees. Mince the remaining cilantro sprigs and mint leaves. Spray a shallow roasting pan with vegetable-oil cooking spray. Lay the chicken, skin side up, on the wire rack, and roast for approximately 30 minutes. The chicken is done when an instant-read meat thermometer registers 170 degrees when inserted deeply into a thigh and the juices run clear when the chicken is pierced with a fork. Transfer the chicken to a heated serving platter or 4 heated dinner plates.

Peel the bananas, then split them in half lengthwise. Pour off all but 3 tablespoons of fat from the roasting pan. Place over medium-high heat and add the butter. When the butter melts and begins to sizzle, add the bananas. Sauté over high heat until the bananas begin to brown slightly, about 1 minute. Pour in the coconut sauce and immediately add the chopped cilantro and mint. Scrape the bottom of the roasting pan to incorporate the pan drippings. Taste and adjust the sauce for seasoning. Spoon the sauce around the chicken and serve at once.

SUGGESTED ACCOMPANIMENTS

Champagne rice pilaf, baby green bean and walnut salad, and fresh strawberry tart *ntensely flavored dishes do not necessarily require lengthy preparation, exotic ingredients, or intricate finishing steps. In this recipe, for example, marinated chicken roasted in a hot oven achieves a new level of gastronomic complexity when napped (coated) with an easy-to-make sauce. Substitutions for key ingredients include replacing the fresh chile with ½ teaspoon Asian chile sauce, using toasted pine nuts in place of the toasted pumpkin seeds, and choosing basil leaves rather than cilantro.*

Serves 4 as an entrée

Tequila Roast Chicken

INGREDIENTS

2 frying chickens, cut into pieces

3 cloves garlic, finely minced

3 serrano chiles, finely minced (including the seeds)

⅓ cup tequila

⅓ cup Dijon mustard

⅓ cup thin soy sauce

2 tablespoons honey

¼ cup finely chopped cilantro sprigs

TEQUILA SAUCE

2 cloves garlic, finely minced

1 serrano chile, finely minced (including the seeds)

2 tablespoons olive oil

1 cup chicken stock

2 tablespoons oyster sauce

1 tablespoon cornstarch

¼ cup tequila

3 ounces crumbled goat cheese

¼ cup salted toasted pumpkin seeds

¼ cup cilantro sprigs

ADVANCE PREPARATION

Rinse the chicken with cold water, then pat dry. In a bowl that is large enough to hold the chicken, combine the garlic, serrano chiles, tequila, mustard, soy sauce, honey, and cilantro. Mix well and add the chicken. Stir to coat the chicken, cover, and refrigerate for at least 15 minutes but not longer than 8 hours.

To make the Tequila Sauce, combine the garlic, serrano chile, and olive oil, then set aside. In a small bowl, combine the chicken stock, oyster sauce, and cornstarch, then set aside. Set aside the tequila, goat cheese (refrigerated), and pumpkin seeds in separate containers. *All advance preparation may be completed up to 8 hours before you begin the final cooking steps.*

FINAL COOKING STEPS

Finely chop the cilantro sprigs and set aside. Preheat the oven to 425 degrees. Line a shallow roasting pan with aluminum foil, and top the roasting pan with a wire rack that has been sprayed with vegetable-oil cooking spray. Place the chicken, skin side up, on the wire rack. Roast the chicken for approximately 30 to 40 minutes. The chicken is done when an instant-read meat thermometer registers 155 degrees for chicken breasts and 170 degrees for thighs and drumsticks and the juices run clear when the chicken is pierced with a fork.

Transfer the chicken to a heated serving platter or 4 heated dinner plates. Place a 12-inch skillet or sauté pan over high heat. Add the garlic, chiles, and olive oil. When the garlic begins to sizzle but before it turns brown, add the chicken stock mixture and bring it to a low boil. Stir in the tequila. Taste and adjust the seasoning, then spoon the sauce around the chicken pieces. Sprinkle the goat cheese, pumpkin seeds, and cilantro over the chicken and sauce, and serve at once.

SUGGESTED ACCOMPANIMENTS

Warm tortillas, watermelon salad, and apple fritters

Hot Chicken Through the Ages

Few other creatures have been so immortalized by poets, studied by writers, appreciated by children, or made the centerpiece of culinary triumphs as the chicken. Historically, cocks were considered birds of beauty, power, virility, and magic. The Greek writer Aelian wrote, "The cock is endowed with surpassing beauty," and Aristophanes noted its regal qualities, saying, "Just like the great king he struts along." But it wasn't just its beauty or presence that garnered recognition. Consider, for instance, that the crowing of a cock was believed to be powerful enough to splinter wood, and that by accurately observing a rooster's eating habits, it was thought that seers could predict the outcome of military campaigns, famines, and the coming of rain. At the same time, the hen became a symbol of motherhood, as was evidenced when the poet Oppian wrote, in the second century BC, "With how much love the playful hen nourishes her tender young ones! If she sees a hawk descending, cackling in a loud voice, she spreads her swelling wings over the clucking chicks."

The chicken has also been valued for its healing properties through the ages. A person suffering from almost any malady, such as a cough, epilepsy, melancholy, fever, or dysentery, looked first to chicken. The sixteenth-century Italian, Ulisse Aldrovandi, in his nine-volume treatise on animals, captured the long-standing universal feeling about chicken when he wrote, "It is clear to all, how much benefit the cock and his wives provide for the human race. They furnish food for both humans who are well and those who are ill and rally those who are almost dead. Which condition of the body, internal or external, does not obtain its remedies from the chicken?"

Originating from jungle fowl thousands of years ago and initially domesticated in India, Southeast Asia, and China, the chicken played an important role in early history. By the fourteenth century BC, the Egyptians, in order to feed the massive labor force building the pyramids, built brick incubators whose fires, kept at a constant 105 degrees, incubated 10,000 eggs at a time. Only in the last eighty years has it been possible to incubate a larger number of eggs at one time. Similarly, the Chinese during the building of the Great Wall in the third century BC, developed methods for the mass incubation of eggs, as well as ways to preserve eggs indefinitely either in brine or by coating them with a mixture of lime and ash.

Chicken spread to Greece, then to Rome, where laws were passed forbidding "the serving of any fowl except a single hen not fattened for the purpose." But while fattening a hen, which was viewed as an effeminate practice, might be illegal, one contemporary Roman writer observed knowingly, "The hen is easily fattened with sweetened meal; it fattens also in the dark. Gluttony is ingenious." Roman soldiers introduced chicken to the rest of Europe. In the fifteenth century, the Spanish and Portuguese sailors brought chickens to the Caribbean and Mexico. Scientists argue whether chickens were indigenous to the New World, but recent evidence indicates that chicken was domesticated, long before the arrival of Columbus, by the Incas and other peoples of South America. The Araucana chickens, common in the Andes and unique among the chickens of the world for laying blue and green eggs, caused comment among many of the early European settlers. In 1590, a Jesuit missionary wrote, "I must say I was astonished at the fowls, which without a doubt were kept even before the coming of the Spaniards."

By the nineteenth century, global trade sparked an unprecedented "chicken mania" in England and America. Chinese chickens, especially the Cochin breed, with their white feathers, black meat and bones, rose-colored combs, and feathered shanks, were introduced to England in 1834 and caused such a sensation that an exhibit of them in Birmingham attracted tens of thousands of people. A nineteenth-century British authority on chickens, S. H. Lewer, said, "Every visitor went home to tell of the new and wonderful fowls, which were as big as ostriches, and roared like lions, while gentle as lambs; which could be kept anywhere, even in a garret, and took to petting like tame cats....Their introduction was the most memorable event that has ever happened in the poultry world; there has been nothing like it before or since."

In the Boston Poultry Show of 1849, more than 10,000 spectators filed through the Public Garden to see the Chinese breeds and other varieties of chicken. A visitor wrote to a friend, "One tent was one hundred and forty-four feet long, by one hundred and fifty wide, filled completely with cages, reserving room enough for the people to walk. It was indeed a magnificent exhibition." Every farm had its flocks of chickens, and every farmer strived to develop new, prize-winning breeds. The best birds went to regional and national exhibitions, in much the same manner as dogs and cats are exhibited today. Hardly a month passed without someone claiming to have produced a new breed. At the shows, chickens were washed with soap and water, rinsed in three tubs of clear water, then toweled off. Exhibition fowl had to be taught "the art of showing themselves to the best advantage and to assume various poses to display her best points." The newspapers were full of breathless accounts of "rare and curious and inexpressibly beautiful examples" of chickens, who, according to well-known breeder George Burnham, had until then "been unknown, unhonored and unsung."

Beginning in the 1890s, industrialization transformed the chicken farm. Between 1899 and 1909, poultry produced in the United States increased by 48 percent, with poultry production concentrated in the Middle Atlantic states and in Ohio, Iowa, Illinois, Missouri, and California. By the early twentieth century, the value of poultry was second only to corn as a revenue-producing agricultural crop. Eighty-eight percent of all farms kept chickens, and of those there were an average of 80.4 chickens per farm. Sixty-five colleges and experimental stations were conducting research in poultry husbandry, and farmers had available sixty-one journals devoted exclusively to poultry.

In the sixteenth century, Henry IV of France said, "If God grants me the usual length of life, I hope to make France so prosperous that every peasant will have a chicken in his pot on Sunday." In 1928, the Republican party echoed this promise with a similar pledge. But it was not until the 1950s that refinements in genetics, immunology, and mechanization at last transformed the chicken from a "free and lively creature," a magical bird and grand announcer of each morning's activities, into an everyday food. Now the chicken has moved from the courtyard to the table, where its culinary adaptability makes it an endlessly fascinating main dish night after night.

"...I hope to make France so prosperous that every peasant will have a chicken in his pot on Sunday."

— Henry IV
Sixteenth century
King of France

Hot Chicken Bubbling in Pots

Chicken bubbling in a pot perfumes the home with enticing aromas. The recipes in this chapter include chicken simmered with shiitake and portobello mushrooms, chicken glazed in a rich balsamic vinegar sauce, and chicken accented with the Caribbean seasonings of nutmeg and chiles. We'll also tell you how to combine chicken with the famous Mexican combination of chiles and chocolate, the easy steps for making an authentic Indian "curry" that is vastly better than the timid American version, and give you three great chicken and rice recipes.

Braising, or cooking in liquid, is the cooking technique used in this chapter. After a few simple preparatory steps, braising sets the cook free for the remainder of the cooking time. Although "braising" and "stewing" are used interchangeably for simmering tough cuts of beef, lamb, and pork until they become tender, chicken is not usually "stewed." Because most chickens sold by supermarkets are tender broiler-fryers, prolonged cooking will result in dry chicken. Unless you have access to stewing hens, chicken should be braised just until cooked through to the center. Use a heavy 12- or 14-inch pan with 3-inch sides and a tight-fitting top. You can braise either skin-on or skinless chicken breasts, thighs, and legs, though the fat from the skin will add flavor to the sauce.

Successful braising involves several important steps. First, preheat the pan until it becomes very hot. Next, season the chicken with salt, pepper, or other seasonings, then sprinkle the chicken on both sides with flour, cornstarch, or bread crumbs. This coating prevents the oil from splattering. Immediately shake off all excess flour. Add the cooking oil to the pan and, when hot, cook the chicken pieces on both sides until golden. Browning the chicken renders the fat, crisps the skin, intensifies the flavor of the sauce, and locks flavor inside each piece. After adding the liquid, regulate the heat so a few bubbles rise steadily to the surface, and cover the pot. Be sure the liquid does not boil, or the chicken will become dry and tasteless. Simmer the chicken on the stovetop or in a 325-degree oven just until an instant-read meat thermometer reads 160 degrees when inserted deeply into the chicken and the juices run clear when pierced with a fork, or, if using a stewing hen, until the meat is tender. When the chicken is cooked, remove the pot from the heat. Let sit 1 minute, then, using strips of paper towels, blot the surface of the liquid until no more fat is visible. (This is done because fat on a sauce masks the underlying flavors.)

Braised chicken dishes using breasts, or a combination of breasts and thighs, taste best if made and served immediately rather than being made a day in advance, refrigerated, and then reheated. Complete the braising 30 minutes before your guests arrive and set the pot aside at room temperature. Serve the chicken within 1 hour by gently reheating it for approximately 5 minutes. If using only thighs, because they have

better marbling than breasts, you may cook the dish a day in advance, refrigerate it, and then reheat it without any deterioration in quality. Thus, substitute chicken thighs for breasts in any of the braised recipes if you want to cook the dish a day in advance.

Chicken with Rosemary-Merlot Sauce

All the winter root vegetables, such as baby beets, parsnips, turnips, carrots, potatoes, and even radishes, are wonderful simmered in a rich sauce. The following recipe uses many of these vegetables, but every time we serve this dish, dinner guests always hunt for the baby beets. Golden and red baby beets the size of a Ping-Pong ball are now sold by most supermarkets. Just trim off the ends, scrub the beets well (they don't need to be peeled), add them to your favorite stew, and watch the reaction of your dinner guests.

Serves 4 as an entrée

INGREDIENTS

2 frying chickens, cut into pieces
Salt and black pepper
½ cup all-purpose flour
¼ cup cooking oil
8 cloves garlic, minced
16 baby red or golden beets
16 baby red potatoes
5 baby turnips
10 baby carrots
4 baby artichokes
10 pearl onions (optional)
⅓ cup chopped parsley

SAUCE

3 cups Merlot or other dry red wine
1 cup chicken stock
¼ cup hoisin sauce
2 tablespoons oyster sauce
1 tablespoon tomato paste
½ teaspoon Asian chile sauce
2 tablespoons finely chopped fresh rosemary

ADVANCE PREPARATION

Rinse the chicken with cold water, then pat dry, cover, and refrigerate. Set the salt, pepper, and flour aside. Set the cooking oil and the garlic aside in separate containers. Scrub the beets, then cut off and discard their ends. Scrub the potatoes, turnips, and carrots. Cut each artichoke in half and scrape away the thistle. Wash, peel, and trim the onions. Cover and set the vegetables aside. Set aside parsley. In a small bowl, combine all ingredients for the sauce. *All advance preparation may be completed up to 8 hours before you begin the final cooking steps.*

FINAL COOKING STEPS

Place a 14-inch skillet or sauté pan over medium-high heat. Place the chicken on a baking sheet or on a piece of waxed or parchment paper. Season the chicken with a sprinkling of salt and black pepper, then flour the chicken on all sides. Shake each piece to remove all excess flour. Add the cooking oil to the pan, and when it becomes hot, add the chicken, skin side up. Regulating the heat so that the oil sizzles but never smokes, cook the chicken on both sides until golden, a total of about 8 minutes.

Remove the chicken from the pan. Pour out all but 2 tablespoons of the oil. Add the garlic and sauté for 15 seconds; then return the chicken, skin side up, to the pan. Add the root vegetables and pour in the wine mixture. Bring the mixture to a low boil, reduce the heat to simmer, cover the pan, and simmer the chicken for about 15 minutes. The chicken is done when an instant-read meat thermometer registers 170 degrees when inserted deeply into a chicken thigh and the juices run clear when the chicken is pierced with a fork.

Transfer the chicken to a heated serving platter or 4 heated dinner plates. Taste the root vegetables. If not tender, continue simmering in the sauce. When tender, remove the pan from the heat. Dab up all oil floating on the sauce with strips of paper towels. Taste and adjust the sauce's seasoning. Spoon the sauce and vegetables around the chicken, sprinkle with the chopped parsley, and serve at once.

SUGGESTED ACCOMPANIMENTS

Grilled polenta, Southwest Caesar salad, and hot apple crumble

*R*ice and chicken, cooked together in one pot, make culinary sense because the rice and the chicken both cook to perfection in the same amount of time. The rice absorbs the flavors of the chicken, and any vegetable or seasoning added to the pot will contribute other layers of taste to both rice and chicken. Once the chicken and rice are combined and the pot is covered, either simmer the dish over the lowest heat on the stovetop, or place it in a preheated 325-degree oven. This dish is a festival of Caribbean and Asian flavors.

Serves 4 as an entrée

Festival Chicken

INGREDIENTS

2 frying chickens, cut into pieces

Salt and pepper

½ cup unbleached all-purpose flour

¼ cup olive oil

¼ cup very finely minced ginger

1 yellow onion, chopped

2 vine-ripened tomatoes, seeded and chopped

1 large yam

1 green bell pepper

1½ cups long-grain white rice (not Minute Rice)

2 cups chicken stock

2 teaspoons finely minced orange zest

1 cup freshly squeezed orange juice

¼ cup Grand Marnier

2 tablespoons thin soy sauce

1 tablespoon Caribbean or Asian chile sauce

1 tablespoon packed light brown sugar

1 teaspoon ground allspice

½ teaspoon ground cinnamon

½ cup lightly packed mint leaves

ADVANCE PREPARATION

Rinse the chicken with cold water, then pat dry, cover, and refrigerate. In separate containers, set aside the salt, pepper, flour, and olive oil. In a bowl, combine the ginger, onion, and tomatoes. Peel the yam, cut it into 4 strips lengthwise, then cut across the strips to make ½-inch cubes. Stem, derib, and seed the pepper, then cut it into ½-inch squares. Add the yam and pepper to the bowl containing the onion and tomatoes. Place the rice in a fine-meshed sieve and rinse with cold water until the rinse water is no longer cloudy, then drain thoroughly. In a bowl, combine the stock, minced orange zest, orange juice, Grand Marnier, soy sauce, chile sauce, sugar, allspice, and cinnamon. Set aside the mint leaves. *All advance preparation may be completed up to 8 hours before you begin the final cooking steps.*

FINAL COOKING STEPS

Finely chop the mint leaves and set aside. Place a 14-inch skillet or sauté pan over medium-high heat. Place the chicken on a baking sheet or on a layer of waxed paper or parchment paper. Season the chicken with salt, then flour the chicken on all sides. Shake each piece to remove all excess flour. Add the cooking oil and, when the oil is hot, add the chicken. Regulating the heat so that the oil constantly sizzles but never smokes, brown the chicken on both sides until golden, a total of about 8 minutes.

Remove the chicken from the pan. Add the ginger, onion, tomatoes, yam, and green pepper, reduce the heat to medium, and sauté until the onion is translucent, about 10 minutes.

Return the chicken to the pan. Add the rice, then pour in the chicken stock mixture. Bring the liquid to a low boil, then reduce the heat to low, cover the pan, and simmer 25 minutes. At this point the rice should be tender, and an instant-read meat thermometer should register 170 degrees when inserted deeply into a chicken thigh and the juices should run clear when the chicken is pierced with a fork. Transfer the chicken to a heated platter or 4 heated plates. Stir the mint into the rice. Taste and adjust the seasoning, then spoon the rice around the chicken and serve at once.

SUGGESTED ACCOMPANIMENTS

Butter lettuce salad, crusty bread, and hot plum pie

Tips on Buying

Throughout the twentieth century, poultry farming grew from small individual farms that provided chicken to nearby towns and cities to today's poultry-industry giants that ship millions of chickens across the country. These mass-produced chickens are raised in densely crowded pens, given antibiotics, fed a diet that includes animal fat and by-products, processed in giant facilities, and then cut, wrapped in plastic, and shipped to market. Until recently, poultry could be frozen to 1 degree Fahrenheit and still be labeled as fresh.

Marvelously convenient and always inexpensive, this mass-produced food has a cost: the disappearance of flavor and texture. Always buy fresh rather than frozen chicken, because the freezing process severely affects flavor and texture. Buy locally raised fresh chicken rather than "fresh" chicken shipped from a distant state. Buy chicken that has been shipped on ice to the market and is displayed open in a meat case instead of being tightly wrapped in plastic trays. The old-fashioned, open arrangement of chicken allows you to pick each piece and ensures that the chicken does not remain in contact with blood and fluid that seeps from the flesh. Buy chickens fed a vegetarian diet. The best-tasting chickens are fed whole grains such as corn and soybeans with no animal fat, animal by-products, or antibiotics mixed into the feed as is done by the large producers (the "hormone-free" claim by producers is meaningless since hormones have not been used anywhere in the poultry industry for over thirty-five years). Buy free-range chickens, which have had access to an outdoor pen or have had a greater area to move within an indoor environment. This results in firmer textured meat. Finally, buy chickens that are processed using cold-chilling systems, which reduces bacterial contamination. Some processors, for example, use a European air-chilling system, and kosher chickens are processed in constantly flowing cold water to reduce bacterial contamination caused by traditional warm-water processing baths. Some of the best chicken producers are Empire Kosher Chicken (Pennsylvania), Rocky Range Chicken (California), Bell & Evans Chicken (Pennsylvania), La Bell Rouge Chicken (Kentucky), and D'Artagnan Chicken (Pennsylvania).

Types of Chicken

POUSSINS: These young chickens, 4 to 6 weeks old, weighing $3/4$ to $1\frac{1}{4}$ pounds, are the most tender and juicy of all chickens. Making beautiful individual servings, they are great roasted whole or split and broiled or barbecued.

BROILER-FRYERS: These young, tender chickens, about 7 weeks old, weighing $2\frac{1}{2}$ to 5 pounds, are the most common type of chicken. Excellent barbecued, grilled, roasted, broiled, sautéed, stir-fried, or braised in liquid, broiler-fryers are sold whole, split in halves, or cut into pieces.

YOUNG ROASTERS: Large meaty birds, 3 to 5 months old and weighing 5 to 8 pounds, these are best roasted or braised because they are less tender than broiler-fryers.

CAPONS: Castrated roosters about 8 months old and weighing approximately 9 pounds, capons have more fat under the skin, so their meat is especially tender and flavorful. They are best roasted.

STEWING CHICKENS: Mature female chickens more than 10 months old and weighing 4 to 5 pounds, these need to be simmered in liquid until tender.

Hot Chicken Sage Advice

No matter how little oil is used to brown chicken, or how deeply golden the skin becomes, a thin layer of fat will often float to the surface at the end of the braising process. Unless this is removed, an oily layer will coat your taste buds and the marvelous layering of flavors will be masked. Just before serving any braised dish, remove the pot from the heat for 1 minute. Dab the surface of the liquid with strips of paper towels to absorb every speck of fat. Bring the liquid to a simmer and make any final seasoning adjustments.

Serves 4 as an entrée

Mushroom Fantasy Chicken

I N G R E D I E N T S

8 chicken breast halves, bone in and skin on

Salt and black pepper

1 tablespoon dried thyme

1/2 cup unbleached all-purpose flour

1/4 cup olive oil

4 cloves garlic, finely minced

3 shallots, minced

1 pound assorted firm mushrooms (such as shiitakes, portobellos, morels, and chanterelles)

1 1/2 cups chicken stock

1/2 cup heavy cream

1/2 cup dry white wine or dry vermouth

2 tablespoons oyster sauce

1 tablespoon tomato paste

1/8 teaspoon ground white pepper

2 tablespoons minced fresh thyme

4 whole green onions (optional)

Zest from 1 lemon (optional)

ADVANCE PREPARATION

Wash the chicken with cold water, then pat dry. Using poultry shears or a heavy knife, trim away all exposed rib bone ends and the wing sockets. Cover and refrigerate the chicken. Set aside separately the salt, pepper, dried thyme, flour, and the oil. In a small bowl, combine the garlic and shallots.

If using shiitake or portobello mushrooms, cut off and discard the stems; cut shiitake caps into quarters and cut portobello caps in half, then cut each half into narrow wedges. Cut morels in half. Cut chanterelles into 1/4-inch-wide slices. Set the mushrooms aside. In a bowl, combine the chicken stock, cream, wine, oyster sauce, tomato paste, pepper, and thyme. Trim the green onions and set aside. Also set aside the lemon zest. *All advance preparation may be completed up to 8 hours before you begin the final cooking steps.*

FINAL COOKING STEPS

Place a 14-inch skillet or sauté pan over medium-high heat. Place the chicken on a baking sheet and season it with salt and freshly ground black pepper. Flour the chicken on all sides and shake each piece to remove all excess flour. Add the cooking oil to the pan and, when the oil is hot, add the chicken skin side up. Regulating the heat so that the oil sizzles but never smokes, cook the chicken for about 5 minutes, then turn the chicken over (skin side down) and cook until the skin is a golden brown, about 5 more minutes.

Remove the chicken. Add the garlic and shallots, sauté for 15 seconds, then add the mushrooms. Sauté the mushrooms until they begin to wilt slightly, about 4 minutes. Remove the mushrooms, return the chicken to the pan, breast side up, scatter the mushrooms around the chicken, and pour in the sauce. Bring the sauce to a low boil, cover the pan, reduce the heat to a simmer, and cook the chicken for about 15 minutes, regulating the heat so that the chicken gently simmers, but never boils. The chicken is done when an instant-read meat thermometer registers 155 degrees when inserted deeply into a breast and the juices run clear when the chicken is pierced with a fork. Transfer the chicken to a heated serving platter or 4 heated dinner plates. Dab up any oil floating on the sauce with strips of paper towels. Turn the heat to high, bring the mushroom sauce to a rapid boil and cook until the sauce begins to thicken, about 2 minutes. Taste and adjust the seasoning. Spoon the mushroom sauce around the chicken, sprinkle with the parsley, and serve at once.

SUGGESTED ACCOMPANIMENTS

Steamed asparagus, warm crusty bread, chilled artichokes, and baked apple pie

Chicken with Balsamic Vinegar

Always taste and adjust the seasoning of a dish just prior to serving it. For all braised dishes, if the sauce is characterless, add one or more of the ingredients used to season the liquid (just adding a little salt is often all that is required). Or, concentrate the flavors by first removing the chicken from the liquid, and absorbing all the oil floating on the surface with strips of paper towels. Then boil the liquid over high heat to reduce it until it achieves the concentrated flavor impact you desire. Spoon the sauce over the chicken and serve it forth. This reduction technique works wonders in this recipe.

Serves 4 as an entrée

INGREDIENTS

8 chicken breast halves, bone in and skin on

Salt to taste

1 teaspoon crushed red pepper (chile flakes)

1 cup finely ground dried unseasoned bread crumbs

¼ cup olive oil

3 cloves garlic, finely minced

2 tablespoons very finely minced ginger

2 cups pearl onions

2 bunches baby carrots

1 cup freshly squeezed orange juice

½ cup balsamic vinegar

¼ cup honey

¼ cup thin soy sauce

1 teaspoon Asian chile sauce

¼ cup finely chopped basil leaves

ADVANCE PREPARATION

Rinse the chicken with cold water, then pat dry. Using poultry shears or a heavy knife, trim away any exposed rib bones, and cut away the wing sockets. Cover and refrigerate the chicken. Set aside the salt, chile, bread crumbs, and oil. In a small bowl, combine the garlic and ginger. Peel the onions. Trim the stem ends from the carrots and peel or scrub the carrots. Combine the vegetables and set aside. In a small bowl, combine the orange juice, balsamic vinegar, honey, soy sauce, and chile sauce and set aside. *All advance preparation may be completed up to 8 hours before you begin the final cooking steps.*

FINAL COOKING STEPS

Finely chop the basil leaves and set aside. Place a 14-inch skillet or sauté pan over medium-high heat. Place the chicken on a baking sheet or on a sheet of waxed paper or parchment paper. Season the chicken with a sprinkling of salt and chile, then sprinkle the bread crumbs on all sides of the chicken. Add the olive oil to the pan and when the oil is hot, add the chicken breasts, skin side up. Regulating the heat so that the oil constantly sizzles but never smokes, cook the chicken for 5 minutes, turn the breasts skin side down, and continue cooking the chicken until the skin is golden, about 5 more minutes of cooking.

Remove the chicken from the pan. Pour out all but 2 tablespoons of the cooking oil, then return the pan to medium-high heat. Add the garlic and ginger, and sauté for 15 seconds, then add the chicken pieces, skin side up. Sprinkle the onions and baby carrots over the chicken and pour in the sauce. Bring the sauce to a low boil, cover the pan, reduce the heat to low, and simmer the chicken for about 15 minutes. The chicken is done when an instant-read meat thermometer registers 155 degrees when inserted deeply into a chicken breast and the juices run clear when the chicken is pierced with a fork.

Transfer the chicken, onions, and carrots to a heated serving platter or 4 heated dinner plates. Temporarily remove the pan from the heat. Dab up any oil floating on the sauce with strips of paper towels. Turn the heat to high, and boil the sauce vigorously until it thickens enough to lightly glaze a spoon, about 4 minutes. Taste the sauce and adjust the seasoning. Pour the sauce through a strainer over the chicken, then sprinkle with the basil. Serve at once.

SUGGESTED ACCOMPANIMENTS

Garlic mashed potatoes, Bibb lettuce salad with walnut oil, and blueberry cheese cake

Firecracker Chicken with Thai Red Curry

A world of flavor is present in Thai red curry paste, which is available at most Asian markets. Because the quality varies greatly from brand to brand, buy Mae Anong Jittritham brand, sold in 17-ounce plastic bags, or Pa Siam Red Curry Paste brand, sold in 14-ounce red plastic containers. Red curry paste keeps perfectly in the refrigerator for several months. Use it as a flavor resource. Add a small amount to a tomato sauce, bubbling on the stove, mash it with avocado when making guacamole, use it as a garnish for a cream of mussel soup, or brush it on hot flour tortillas to fill with a stir-fry.

Serves 4 as an entrée

INGREDIENTS

4 chicken legs

4 chicken thighs

Salt and freshly ground black pepper

½ cup unbleached all-purpose flour

¼ cup cooking oil

4 cloves garlic, minced

2 tablespoons very finely minced ginger

1 cup coconut milk

½ cup chicken stock

½ cup Chinese rice wine or dry sherry

2 tablespoons Thai fish sauce

¼ cup Thai red curry paste

¼ cup cilantro sprigs

1 lime

ADVANCE PREPARATION

Rinse the chicken with cold water, pat dry, cover, and refrigerate. In separate containers, set aside the salt, pepper, flour, and cooking oil. Combine the garlic and ginger and set aside. In a small bowl, combine the coconut milk, stock, rice wine, and fish sauce. Set aside separately the red curry paste and cilantro.

Place a 12-inch skillet or sauté pan over medium-high heat. Place the chicken on a baking sheet, season with salt and freshly ground black pepper, then sprinkle the flour on all sides of the chicken. Shake each piece to remove all excess flour. Add the cooking oil to the pan and, when the oil is hot, add the chicken. Regulating the heat so that the oil sizzles but never smokes, cook the pieces on all sides until golden, a total of about 8 minutes.

Remove the chicken from the pan. Return the pan to medium-high heat, add the garlic and ginger to the sauté pan and cook until the seasonings begin to sizzle, about 1 minute. Add the red curry paste, sauté for 1 minute, then add the coconut mixture, and return the chicken, skin side up, to the pan. Bring the sauce to a low boil, cover the pan, and reduce the heat to low. Regulating the heat so that the chicken gently simmers, but never boils, cook the chicken until it is tender, about 20 minutes. The chicken is done when an instant-read meat thermometer registers 170 degrees when inserted deeply into a thigh and the juices run clear when the chicken is pierced with a fork. Refrigerate if preparing more than 1 hour ahead. *All advance preparation may be completed up to 8 hours before you begin the final cooking steps.*

FINAL COOKING STEPS

Finely chop the cilantro. Cut the lime into quarters. Reheat the sauce and chicken. Taste and adjust the seasoning. Transfer the chicken to a heated serving platter or 4 heated dinner plates. Dab up any oil floating on the sauce with strips of paper towels. Spoon the sauce over the chicken. Garnish with chopped cilantro and lime quarters. Serve at once.

SUGGESTED ACCOMPANIMENTS

Pad Thai noodle salad and Key lime pie

This recipe gains its special flavor from curry paste. "Curry" means a blend of spices that become the dominant flavor element in whatever dishes in which it is used. Thai cooks make several types of curry pastes, including red curry pastes using dried red chiles, and green curry paste made from basil and cilantro. But to most Westerners, curry means a powder made from cumin, coriander, fenugreek, chiles, and turmeric. This type of "curry powder" was invented by the British in India to approximate the blends of seasonings that Indian cooks grind as needed and which vary depending on the dish and the whim of the cook. Since our "Indian" curry powders are often stale, this book shows you the simple method for making a far more flavorful curry paste. It lasts for months in the refrigerator.

Bombay Chicken

Serves 4 as an entrée

INGREDIENTS

8 chicken thighs, skinned and boned

Indian Curry Paste (see page 43)

3 tablespoons cooking oil

2 yellow onions, chopped

8 small red potatoes, quartered

8 carrots, peeled and cut in 1-inch pieces

1 cup dark raisins

2 cups chicken stock

1 cup coconut milk

1 cup unsweetened slivered coconut

1 cup sliced almonds

1/4 cup cilantro sprigs

PICKLE RELISH

1/2 hothouse cucumber

1 teaspoon salt

1/2 cup unseasoned rice vinegar

1/4 cup sugar

1/4 teaspoon Asian chile sauce

ADVANCE PREPARATION

Preheat the oven to 325 degrees to toast the nuts. Rinse the chicken with cold water, then pat dry. Cut the chicken meat into pieces about 2 inches long and 1 inch thick. Make the Indian Curry Paste, then in a small bowl combine the curry paste and chicken. Mix well to coat the chicken. Cover and refrigerate for at least 15 minutes but not longer than 8 hours. Combine and set aside the cooking oil and onions. Combine the potatoes, carrots, and raisins and set aside. Combine the stock and coconut milk and set aside.

In a 10-inch skillet or sauté pan over medium heat, toast the coconut until golden. Place the almonds on a baking sheet and toast in the preheated oven until golden, about 12 minutes. In separate containers, set the coconut, almonds, and cilantro aside.

To make the pickle relish, cut the cucumber in half and scoop away the seeds. Cut the cucumber crosswise into 1/8-inch-wide pieces. Sprinkle evenly with the salt and set aside for 1 hour. Meanwhile, in a small saucepan, combine the vinegar, sugar, and chile sauce. Bring to a low boil, reduce the heat to low, and simmer for 5 minutes, then transfer to a bowl. Let cool to room temperature. Rinse the cucumber with cold water, pat dry, and combine with the vinegar mixture. Let marinate for at least 1 hour (the pickles can be made several days in advance and refrigerated in the pickling liquid).

Place a 14-inch skillet or sauté pan over medium-high heat and when hot add the cooking oil and onions. Sauté the onion until it begins to turn golden, about 10 minutes. Add the chicken-curry paste combination. Sauté the chicken until it loses its raw exterior color. Add the potatoes, carrots, raisins, and chicken stock. Bring the sauce to a low simmer, cover the pan, and simmer until the potatoes are tender, about 15 minutes. Set the dish aside at room temperature if reheating the dish within 1 hour, otherwise refrigerate. *All advance preparation may be completed up to a day before you begin the final cooking steps.*

FINAL COOKING STEPS

Chop the cilantro. Place the sauté pan over medium-high heat and bring the curry to a low boil. Taste and adjust the seasoning. Transfer the chicken and vegetables to a heated platter or 4 heated dinner plates. Dab up any oil floating on the sauce with strips of paper towels. Spoon the sauce over the chicken and vegetables. Add the cilantro. Serve at once, along with containers of toasted coconut, toasted almonds, and the pickle relish.

SUGGESTED ACCOMPANIMENTS

Tomato and basil salad and mango sorbet with fudge sauce

Moroccan Chicken with Olives and Saffron

INGREDIENTS

2 frying chickens, cut into pieces

2 teaspoons ground cinnamon

Salt

½ cup unbleached all-purpose flour

1 cup olives, European low brine, pitted

½ cup pine nuts

4 cloves garlic, finely minced

2 tablespoons very finely minced ginger

1½ cups white long-grain rice (not Minute Rice)

3 cups chicken stock

1 tablespoon minced lemon zest

¼ cup freshly squeezed lemon juice

2 tablespoons honey

2 teaspoons Asian chile sauce

1½ teaspoons salt

½ teaspoon turmeric

2 large pinches saffron threads

½ cup finely chopped cilantro sprigs

1 cup finely chopped fresh parsley

¼ cup olive oil

Brilliantly yellow rice, dark olives, and complex flavors perfectly accent this braised chicken. When using saffron, buy saffron threads, which have better flavor and give a more intense color than powdered saffron. We like to add ½ teaspoon of ground turmeric in order to guarantee an even more vivid yellow. The type of olive chosen is very important for flavor. Purchase cured pitted olives imported from Mediterranean countries and available at gourmet food shops and Greek delicatessens. Don't confuse these olives with American green or black olives, which are mediocre tasting.

Serves 4 as an entrée

ADVANCE PREPARATION

Preheat the oven to 325 degrees (to toast the nuts). Rinse the chicken with cold water, then pat dry, cover, and refrigerate. Divide the cinnamon between 2 containers. In separate containers, set aside the salt, flour, and olives. Place the pine nuts on a baking sheet and toast until golden, about 8 minutes. In a small bowl, combine the garlic and ginger. Place the rice in a fine-meshed sieve, and rinse it with cold water until the rinse water is no longer cloudy; drain thoroughly. In a bowl, combine the stock, minced lemon zest, lemon juice, honey, chile sauce, salt, turmeric, saffron, and half of the cinnamon. *All advance preparation may be completed up to 8 hours before you begin the final cooking steps.*

FINAL COOKING STEPS

Preheat the oven to 325 degrees. In separate containers, set aside the cilantro and parsley. Place a 14-inch skillet or sauté pan over medium-high heat. Place the chicken on a baking sheet or on a piece of waxed paper or parchment paper. Season the chicken with the remaining cinnamon, sprinkle with salt, and coat completely with flour. Shake each piece to remove all excess flour. Add the olive oil to the pan and, when it is hot, add the chicken, skin side up. Regulating the heat so that the oil sizzles but never smokes, cook the chicken on both sides until golden, a total of about 8 minutes.

Remove the chicken from the pan. Place the pan over medium-high heat. Add the garlic and ginger. Sauté for 15 seconds, and add the rice. Sauté the rice for 2 minutes until coated, then add the olives, pine nuts, chicken stock mixture, cilantro, and half of the parsley. Bring the sauce to a low boil, then return the chicken, skin side up, to the pan. Reduce the heat to simmer, cover the pan, and place the pan in the preheated oven for approximately 25 minutes. The dish is done when an instant-read meat thermometer registers 170 degrees when inserted deeply into a chicken thigh, the juices run clear when the chicken is pierced with a fork, and the rice is tender.

Transfer the chicken to a heated serving platter or 4 heated dinner plates. Taste the rice and adjust the seasoning, especially for salt. Spoon the rice around the chicken, sprinkle with the remaining chopped parsley, and serve at once.

SUGGESTED ACCOMPANIMENTS

Tomato, basil, and feta salad and raspberry sorbet with chocolate meltdown sauce

Chicken Mole with Chiles and Chocolate

One of the most famous Mexican dishes, **mole,** or sauce, is more than just a sauce—it's a multiflavored, rich chicken stew made with ground nuts, seeds, herbs, spices, chiles, and, sometimes, chocolate. Varying from cook to cook and simmered in large clay pots that acquire a special patina of flavor, mole is served throughout Mexico in both simple cafes and elegant restaurants (the city of Oaxaca is known for its seven moles). The most famous mole is the dark, chile-chocolate mole from Puebla. Called **mole poblano,** legend holds that it was first created by Sor Andrea for the viceroy of New Spain in the late seventeenth century.

Serves 4 as an entrée

INGREDIENTS

8 chicken thighs

Salt

½ cup unbleached all-purpose flour

¼ cup cooking oil

2 dried pasilla chiles, seeded and stemmed

2 dried ancho chiles, seeded and stemmed

1 chipotle chile in adobo sauce

¼ cup dark raisins

2 tablespoons white sesame seeds, toasted

2 tablespoons almonds, toasted

½ teaspoon coriander seeds

½ teaspoon aniseeds

½-inch cinnamon stick

4 cloves

4 garlic cloves

1 large vine-ripened tomato, seeded

1 ounce Mexican Ibarra chocolate or unsweetened cocoa powder

2 cups chicken stock

¼ cup cilantro sprigs

1 avocado

ADVANCE PREPARATION

Rinse the chicken with cold water, then pat dry. Set aside the salt, flour, and cooking oil. Bring 4 cups of water to a boil in a medium saucepan. Add the dried chiles to the boiling water, remove the saucepan from the heat and cover for 30 minutes. Set aside the chipotle chile. Cover the raisins with hot tap water, let soak for 20 minutes, then discard the water. In a food processor, very finely mince the sesame seeds and almonds, then set aside. To a small skillet or sauté pan, add the coriander, aniseeds, cinnamon stick, and cloves. Place over medium heat and toast until the spices release their fragrance, about 3 minutes. Transfer the spices to a spice grinder and very finely grind. Set aside the garlic. Set aside the tomato. Cut the chocolate into fine pieces and set aside. Set aside the stock.

In a food processor, finely mince the garlic. Add the chiles and very finely mince. Add the ground seeds, nuts, spices, and tomato, and process into a paste. Place a 14-inch skillet or sauté pan over medium-high heat. When hot, add the mole sauce, bring to a low simmer, and sauté for 2 minutes. Add the chicken stock and chocolate, bring to a low boil, cover, reduce heat to low, and simmer 30 minutes. Transfer the mole sauce to a bowl. Clean the sauté pan or skillet and return to medium-high heat. Place the chicken on a baking sheet. Season the chicken with salt, then coat completely with flour. Shake each piece of chicken to remove all excess flour. Add the cooking oil to the pan and when hot, add the chicken, skin side up. Regulating the heat so that the oil sizzles but never smokes, cook the chicken on both sides until golden, a total of about 8 minutes.

Add the mole sauce. Bring to a low boil. Reduce the heat to low and cover the pan. Regulating the heat so that the chicken simmers gently but never boils, cook the chicken thighs until they are tender, about 30 minutes. The chicken is done when an instant-read meat thermometer registers 170 degrees when inserted deeply into a thigh and the juices run clear when the chicken is pierced with a fork. Refrigerate if preparing more than 1 hour ahead. *All advance preparation may be completed up to 8 hours before you begin the final cooking steps.*

FINAL COOKING STEPS

Finely chop the cilantro. Cut the avocado into thin slices. Reheat the sauce and chicken. If the sauce is very thick, thin with a little water or more stock. Taste and adjust the seasoning. Transfer the chicken to a heated serving platter or 4 heated dinner plates. Dab up any oil floating on the sauce with strips of paper towels. Spoon the sauce over the chicken. Garnish with avocado and cilantro. Serve at once.

SUGGESTED ACCOMPANIMENTS

Hot corn tortillas, barbecued corn on the cob, and Kahlúa flan

Southwest Chicken with a Cilantro Accent

This recipe blends the seasonings of ground coriander, cumin, and cinnamon with the smoky, spicy low-note taste from chipotle chiles in adobo sauce, the sweet, acid high-note contribution of vine-ripened tomatoes, and a sour cream accent. To vary the flavor, substitute, for the chipotle chiles, two dried ancho chiles soaked in boiling water until softened, then seeded and finely minced. During the height of the corn season, stir 1 cup fresh raw corn kernels into the simmering sauce during the last 5 minutes of cooking. This adds great color, flavor, and texture.

Serves 4 as an entrée

INGREDIENTS

8 chicken breast halves, bone in and skin on

1 tablespoon ground coriander

1 tablespoon ground cumin

2 teaspoons ground cinnamon

½ cup finely ground cornmeal

¼ cup olive oil

6 cloves garlic, finely minced

1 yellow onion, chopped

1½ pounds vine-ripened tomatoes, seeded and chopped (about 2 cups)

1 cup chicken stock

¼ cup dry red wine

¼ cup chipotle chiles in adobo sauce, puréed

½ teaspoon salt

½ cup sour cream

1 cup lightly packed cilantro sprigs

ADVANCE PREPARATION

Rinse the chicken with cold water, then pat dry. Using poultry shears or a heavy knife, trim away any exposed rib bone ends and cut away the wing sockets, then cover and refrigerate the chicken. In a small bowl, combine the coriander, cumin, and cinnamon; mix well, then divide the mixture equally into 2 small containers. Set the cornmeal aside. Set the olive oil aside. Combine the garlic and onion, then set aside. In a bowl, combine half of the coriander mixture with the chopped tomatoes, chicken stock, red wine, chipotle chiles, and salt. Set aside the sour cream and cilantro in separate containers. *All advance preparation may be completed up to 8 hours before you begin the final cooking steps.*

FINAL COOKING STEPS

Chop the cilantro. Place a 14-inch skillet or sauté pan over medium-high heat. Place the chicken on a baking sheet or on a piece of waxed paper or parchment paper. Season the chicken with the remaining coriander-spice mixture and a sprinkling of salt, then sprinkle the chicken on both sides with cornmeal, shaking each piece to remove any excess cornmeal.

Add the olive oil to the pan, and when it is hot, add the chicken, skin side up. Regulating the heat so that the oil sizzles but never smokes, sauté the chicken for 5 minutes, then turn it skin side down and continue cooking until it is golden, about 5 more minutes.

Remove the chicken from the pan. With the pan still over medium-high heat, add the garlic and onion. Sauté until the onion is translucent, about 6 minutes. Return the chicken to the pan, skin side up. Add the tomato mixture, bring to a low boil, cover the pan, reduce the heat to low, and simmer the chicken for about 15 minutes. The chicken is done when an instant-read meat thermometer registers 155 degrees when inserted deeply into a chicken breast and the juices run clear when the chicken is pierced with a fork.

Transfer the chicken to a heated platter or 4 heated dinner plates. Dab up all fat floating on the surface with strips of paper towels. Turn the heat to high and boil the sauce vigorously until it thickens enough to lightly coat a spoon, about 5 minutes. Taste and adjust the seasoning, especially for salt. Spoon the sauce over the chicken, garnish the chicken with cilantro and sour cream, and serve at once.

SUGGESTED ACCOMPANIMENTS

Corn bread muffins, avocado and papaya salad, and Grand Marnier fudge cake

Many influences were fused to create jambalaya, a dish that epitomizes New Orleans food. When the Spanish arrived in Louisiana, in order to closely duplicate their famous rice dish, paella, they substituted oysters, crawfish, and andouille sausage for the unavailable ingredients of clams, mussels, and ham. The original name, **jambon à la yaya**, is derived from the French word **jambon** for ham, **à la**, French/Acadian for "on" or "with," and the African word **yaya** meaning "rice." In the following version, shrimp shells simmer in the chicken stock to impart a wonderful shellfish flavor.

Serves 4 as an entrée

Chicken Yaya

INGREDIENTS

1 frying chicken, cut into pieces

½ cup unbleached all-purpose flour

¼ cup light olive oil

1 pound medium shrimp in the shell

3 cups chicken stock

4 cloves garlic, finely minced

1 large yellow onion, chopped

1 yellow or red bell pepper, stemmed, seeded, deribbed, and chopped

1 cup seeded and chopped vine-ripened tomato

8 ounces andouille or spicy sausage, thinly sliced

1½ cups long-grain white rice (not Minute Rice)

2 bay leaves

2 tablespoons Worcestershire sauce

1 teaspoon salt

½ teaspoon cayenne powder

½ teaspoon freshly ground black pepper

¼ teaspoon ground cloves

3 tablespoons minced fresh thyme

¼ cup finely chopped basil leaves

½ cup finely chopped fresh parsley

ADVANCE PREPARATION

Rinse the chicken with cold water, then pat dry, cover, and refrigerate. Set aside the flour. Set aside the olive oil. Shell the shrimp, reserving the shells. Butterfly the shrimp by cutting deeply along the top ridge of the shrimp; remove and discard the dark vein. Cover the shrimp and refrigerate. Place the shrimp shells and stock in a medium saucepan, bring to a low boil, reduce the heat to very low, cover the pan, and simmer the stock for 20 minutes. Strain the stock and let cool to room temperature. Discard the shells. Prepare the garlic, onion, pepper, tomato, and sausage, setting these aside together in a bowl. Place the rice in a fine-meshed sieve, rinse the rice with cold water until the water runs clear, then drain the rice and set aside. In a bowl, combine the cooled stock, bay leaves, Worcestershire sauce, salt, cayenne, pepper, cloves, thyme, and basil. *All advance preparation may be completed up to 8 hours before you begin the final cooking steps.*

FINAL COOKING STEPS

Finely chop the parsley and set aside. Preheat the oven to 325 degrees. Place a deep 12- or 14-inch skillet over medium-high heat. Place the chicken on a baking sheet or on a piece of waxed paper or parchment paper. Sprinkle the flour on all sides of the chicken, then shake each piece to remove all excess flour. Add the olive oil to the frying pan and, when hot, add the chicken, skin side up. Regulating the heat so that the chicken sizzles, but the oil never smokes, cook the chicken on both sides until golden, about 8 minutes.

Remove the chicken from the pan. Add the vegetables and sausage, reduce the heat to medium, and sauté the vegetables until the onions are translucent, about 10 minutes. Add the rice and sauté for 2 minutes until heated. Add the chicken stock mixture. Add the chicken, skin side up.

Bring the liquid to a low boil, then cover the pan, and place the pan in the preheated oven. Cook for 25 to 30 minutes. At this point the rice should be tender, and an instant-read meat thermometer should register 170 degrees when inserted deeply into a thigh and the juices should run clear when the chicken is pierced with a fork. During the last 5 minutes of cooking, scatter the shrimp across the rice, recover, and continue cooking. Taste and adjust the seasoning. Transfer the chicken to a heated serving platter or 4 heated dinner plates. Stir the shrimp into the rice, transfer the rice to the platter or plates, sprinkle on the parsley, and serve at once.

SUGGESTED ACCOMPANIMENTS

Dirty rice pilaf and bourbon ice cream with caramel butter sauce

Glossary

CHICKEN STOCK: When homemade chicken stock is unavailable, all the recipes work well using canned low-salt broth. Best brand: Swanson Chicken Broth.

CHILES, FRESH: The smaller the chile, the spicier its taste. Over 80 percent of the heat is concentrated in the ribs and seeds. Because it is a tedious operation to remove the seeds from jalapeño and serrano chiles, we always mince the chiles along with their seeds. Substitute: Your favorite bottled chile sauce.

CHILE SAUCE, ASIAN, CARIBBEAN, OR LOUISIANA: This is a general term for the countless varieties of chile and hot pepper sauces from around the world. Use your own favorite chile sauce and vary the amount depending on personal preference. Most of the recipes designate Asian chile sauce. Best Brand: Rooster Brand Delicious Hot Chile Garlic Sauce, sold in 8-ounce clear plastic jars with a green cap. Refrigerate after opening. Substitute: One or more fresh jalapeño or serrano chiles.

CHIPOTLE CHILES IN ADOBO SAUCE: Smoked, dried jalapeños that are stewed in a tomato-vinegar-garlic sauce, chipotle chiles in adobo sauce are available in 4-ounce cans at all Mexican markets and many supermarkets. To use, purée the chiles with the adobo sauce in a blender or electric mini-chopper. It is unnecessary to remove the seeds. Substitute: None.

CITRUS JUICE AND ZEST: Freshly squeezed citrus juice has a sparkling fresh taste completely absent from all store-bought juices. Because its flavor deteriorates quickly, always squeeze citrus juice within hours of use and keep it covered and refrigerated. When a recipe calls for finely minced zest, remove the colored skin of the citrus fruit, leaving the white pith, using a potato peeler or a simple tool called a zester, then finely mince the zest using an electric mini-chopper, rather than grating the citrus with a cheese grater, which is very time-consuming.

COCONUT MILK: Adds flavor and body to sauces. Available canned in Asian markets. Always purchase a Thai brand whose ingredients are just coconut and water. Never buy the "lowfat" coconut milks, because they have a bad taste. Stir the coconut milk before using. Best brand: Chaokoh brand from Thailand. Once opened, store coconut milk covered in the refrigerator for up to 1 week, then discard. Substitute: Half-and-half or chicken stock. If substituting chicken stock, you may want to stir a little cornstarch-water mixture into the soup or sauce just before serving in order to add more body.

COOKING OIL: Use any mild oil with a high smoking temperature, such as peanut oil, safflower oil, or corn oil.

CURRY PASTE: Curry is a blend of many spices. Because commercially made curry powder quickly loses its flavor, whenever possible substitute half the amount of curry paste, which has a far more complex taste. Curry paste is available at most supermarkets, or you can easily make your own by using the Indian Curry Paste recipe on page 43 (in the recipe for Tandoori Chicken).

FISH SAUCE, THAI: Fish sauce, made from fermenting fish in brine, is used in Southeast Asian cooking to add flavor in much the same way as the Chinese use soy sauce. Purchase Thai fish sauce, which has the lowest salt content. Best brand: Three Crab brand or Tiparos brand fish sauce. Substitutes: Thin soy sauce, although the flavor is quite different.

GINGER, FRESH: This pungent and spicy rhizome, grown in Hawaii, is available at virtually all supermarkets in the produce section. Buy firm ginger with a smooth skin. It is unnecessary to peel ginger unless the skin is wrinkled. To use: Because the tough ginger fiber runs lengthwise along the root, always cut ginger crosswise in paper-thin slices, then very finely mince it by hand or in an electric mini-chopper. Store in the refrigerator or at room temperature for up to 1 month. Substitute: None.

HERBS, FRESH AND DRIED: The flavor of all dishes is vastly improved by using fresh rather than dry herbs. Fresh herbs are now available at most supermarkets throughout the year. The stems of most fresh herbs are tough. When using fresh oregano, rosemary, thyme, basil, and mint, strip the leaves off the stems and discard the stems. For parsley, discard all the thick stems. When chopping or mincing cilantro, discard only the bottom portion of stems, then chop or mince the leaves and the upper tender stem.

HOISIN SAUCE: Hoisin sauce, a thick, sweet, spicy, dark condiment, is made with soybeans, chiles, garlic, ginger, and sugar. Once opened, it keeps indefinitely at room temperature. Best brand: Koon Chun Hoisin Sauce.

MUSHROOMS, FRESH: For all recipes in which mushrooms are to be cooked, choose mushrooms with a firm texture, such as buttons, criminis, shiitakes, chanterelles, portobellos, and morels, rather than the flabby-textured enoki and oyster mushrooms.

OLIVE OIL: Unless otherwise specified, use the intensely flavored green-tinted extra virgin olive oil for salad dressings, and the slightly yellow-tinted and very mild-tasting "light" olive oil (often labeled just "olive oil") for dishes in which you don't want a strong olive taste to dominate other flavors.

OYSTER SAUCE: Also called "oyster-flavored sauce," this bottled sauce gives dishes a rich taste without a hint of its seafood origins. Keeps indefinitely in the refrigerator. Substitute: None. Although it is available at almost every supermarket, the following best brands are available mostly at Asian markets: Sa Cheng Oyster Flavored Sauce, Hop Sing Lung Oyster Sauce, and Lee Kum Kee Oyster Flavored Sauce, Premium Brand.

RICE WINE OR DRY SHERRY: Always use good-quality Chinese rice wine or dry sherry. The best brands of rice wine are Pagoda Brand Shao Xing Rice Wine and Pagoda Brand Shao Hsing Hua Tiao Chiew. Substitute: A moderately expensive dry sherry.

SAFFRON: The world's most expensive spice, saffron adds a wonderful yellow tint to sauces, soups and rice dishes. Always purchase saffron threads rather than the less expensive powdered saffron, which lacks both flavor and coloring ability. For the same coloring effect, substitute ½ teaspoon of turmeric powder for 1 large pinch of saffron threads.

SESAME OIL, DARK: A nutty, dark golden brown oil made from crushed toasted sesame seeds. Do not confuse dark sesame oil with the American manufactured clear and tasteless sesame oil, or Chinese black sesame oil, which has a strong, unpleasant taste. Dark sesame oil will last for at least 1 year at room temperature and indefinitely in the refrigerator. Best brand: Kadoya Sesame Oil.

SOY SAUCE, THIN: "Thin" or "light" soy sauce is a watery, mildly salty liquid made from soy beans, roasted wheat, yeast, and salt. If you are concerned about sodium content, reduce the quantity of soy sauce rather than using the inferior tasting, more expensive low-sodium brands. Best Brands: Pearl River Bridge brand Golden Label Superior Soya Sauce, Koon Chun brand Thin Soy Sauce, or Kikkoman Regular Soy Sauce.

SOY SAUCE, DARK: "Dark," "heavy," or "black" soy sauce is thin soy sauce with the addition of molasses, and is used to add a rich flavor and color to sauces, stews, and soups. Never confuse "dark" soy sauce with "thick" soy sauce, which is sold in jars and has a syruplike consistency and an unpleasantly strong taste. Once opened, dark soy sauce keeps indefinitely at room temperature. Best brand: Pearl River Bridge brand Mushroom Soy Sauce.

SPICES, DRIED: Freshly toasted and ground spices have a much more complex flavor than bottled ground spices. In an ungreased skillet placed over medium heat, toast the spice(s) until they release their fragrance, about 2 minutes, then very finely grind them in an electric grinder. Use the same day.

TOMATOES, FRESH, AND TOMATO PASTE: All recipes using tomatoes specify vine-ripened tomatoes. During the months when these are unavailable, substitute hothouse tomatoes. To increase the flavor of hothouse tomatoes, cut the tomatoes into $\frac{1}{4}$-inch-thick slices and broil the tomatoes on both sides until lightly golden, then cut and use as directed in the recipe. In addition, we often add 1 teaspoon of concentrated Italian tomato paste, of which a good brand is Pagani, sold in $4\frac{1}{2}$-ounce tubes.

VINEGAR, BALSAMIC: This vinegar has a nutty, mildly sour and slightly sweet flavor. For the recipes in this book, use a moderately priced balsamic vinegar ($5 for an 8-ounce bottle) available in most supermarkets. An excellent substitute is the Chinese black vinegar labeled Chinkiang Vinegar.

Conversion Charts

LIQUID MEASUREMENTS

Cups and Spoons	Liquid Ounces	Approximate Metric Term	Approximate Centiliters	Actual Milliliters
1 tsp	⅙ oz	1 tsp	½ cL	5 mL
1 Tb	½ oz	1 Tb	1½ cL	15 mL
¼ c; 4 Tb	2 oz	½ dL; 4 Tb	6 cL	59 mL
⅓ c; 5 Tb	2⅔ oz	¾ dL; 5 Tb	8 cL	79 mL
½ c	4 oz	1 dL	12 cL	119 mL
⅔ c	5⅓ oz	1½ dL	15 cL	157 mL
¾ c	6 oz	1¾ dL	18 cL	178 mL
1 c	8 oz	¼ L	24 cL	237 mL
1¼ c	10 oz	3 dL	30 cL	296 mL
1⅓ c	10⅔ oz	3¼ dL	33 cL	325 mL
1½ c	12 oz	3½ dL	35 cL	355 mL
1⅔ c	13⅓ oz	3¾ dL	39 cL	385 mL
1¾ c	14 oz	4 dL	41 cL	414 mL
2 c; 1 pt	16 oz	½ L	47 cL	473 mL
2½ c	20 oz	6 dL	60 cL	592 mL
3 c	24 oz	¾ L	70 cL	710 mL
3½ c	28 oz	⅘ L; 8dL	83 cL	829 mL
4 c; 1 pt	32 oz	1 L	95 cL	946 mL
5 c	40 oz	1¼ L	113 cL	1134 mL
6 c; 1½ qt	48 oz	1½ L	142 cL	1420 mL
8 c; 2 pt	64 oz	2 L	190 cL	1893 mL
10 c; 2½ qt	80 oz	2½ L	235 cL	2366 mL
12 c; 3 qt	96 oz	2¾ L	284 cL	2839 mL
4 qt	128 oz	3¾ L	375 cL	3785 mL
5 qt	4¾ L			
6 qt	5½ L (or 6 L)			
8 qt	7½ L (or 8 L)			

LENGTH

⅛ in	= 3mm
¼ in	= 6mm
⅓ in	= 1 cm
½ in	= 1.5 cm
¾ in	= 2 cm
1 in	= 2.5 cm
1½ in	= 4 cm
2 in	= 5 cm
2½ in	= 6 cm
4 in	= 10 cm
8 in	= 2 cm
10 in	= 25 cm

TEMPERATURES

275°F	= 140°C
300°F	= 150°C
325°F	= 170°C
350°F	= 180°C
375°F	= 190°C
400°F	= 200°C
450°F	= 230°C
475°F	= 240°C
500°F	= 250°C

OTHER CONVERSIONS

Ounces to milliliters: multiply ounces by 29.57

Quarts to liters: multiply quarts by 0.95

Milliliters to ounces: multiply milliliters by 0.034

Liters to quarts: multiply liters by 1.057

Ounces to grams: multiply ounces by 28.3

Grams to ounces: multiply grams by .0353

Pounds to grams: multiply pounds by 453.59

Pounds to kilograms: multiply pounds by 0.45

Ounces to milliliters: multiply ounces by 30

Cups to liters: multiply cups by 0.24

Special thanks to Fillamento Gallery, San Francisco.

Acknowledgments

This cookbook would not be possible without Phil Wood, who, as our publisher and friend, offered enthusiastic encouragement and sage advice throughout the birth of the book. Other key people at Ten Speed Press were Kirsty Melville, who as our editor skillfully guided the proposal from a rough outline to this finished book; Lorena Jones, whose inspired editing and insights improved the text at every juncture; and Jo Ann Deck. We've enjoyed the many hours spent poring over the book's layout with our friend and book designer Beverly Wilson. Her design talent, creativity, and laughter were a wonderful addition to our team. Thanks for sharing our vision.

Many friends helped bring this book into print and we are deeply appreciative for their support. Jack and Dolores Cakebread provided their winery kitchen for testing many of these recipes with a small group of cooking friends. Bettylu Kessler helped with key aspects of completing the manuscript and testing the recipes.

The historical information and quotes about chicken are drawn from a marvelous and definitive book about chicken through the ages, The Chicken Book (Little, Brown, & Company, 1975) by biologist Page Smith and historian Charles Daniel. Harold McGee provided much of the key information about food safety and food science regarding chicken. Allen Shainsky of Petaluma Poultry shared his wealth of knowledge, especially about Rocky Range chickens. Thank you for all your help.

After the recipes were tested at our home and used in cooking classes, they were given a final evaluation by the following home cooks. This book gained much from their special insights. Thank you, Sherry Adkins, Elizabethe Bransteiter, Jane Breed, Jennifer and David Bressie, Lisa Burrell, Joyce Cooper, Kim and George David, Adelle and Joe DiGiorgia, Arleen Dobashi, Carole Dorshkind, Joanne Duffy and Michael Ott, Hal Frank, Joyce Fujiwara, Elijah Garcia, Susan Hartkemeier, Joann Hecht, Linda Hickman, Estelle Hoffman, Marina Hsieh, Kimberly Iavolo, Robin and Ginny Jaquith, Vicky Kell, William and Barbara Kitchens, Mary and Larry Makal, Lorraine McDonnell, Lynne McIntosh, Anne and David McVey, Tim Neenan, Phoebe Olcott, Liz Pompilio, Daniel and Eileen Randall, Gloria Rosland, Kendall Shinn, Betty Snyder, Donyelle Stickel, Phyllis Vaccarelli, Ana Villa, Connie West, Diana Wherrett and Henry Dinsdale, and Hermia Woo.

Index